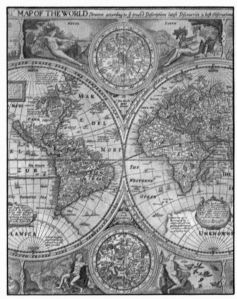

JOURNEYS TO THE FAR WEST

JOURNEYS TO THE FAR WEST

EDWARD CAVELL

James Lorimer & Company, Publishers
Toronto 1979

ISBN 0-88862-270-8 cloth

Design: Don Fernley
Map: Vera Jacyk

6   5   4   3   2   1   79   80   81   82   83   84   85

Canadian Cataloguing in Publication Data

Cavell, Edward, 1948-
    Journeys to the far west

Bibliography: p. IX
ISBN 0-88862-270-8

1. Canada, Western — History.*   2. Canada, Western — Description and travel* — Views.*   I. Title.

FC3217.C38   971.2′02′0222   C79-094481-2
F1060.9.C38

James Lorimer & Company, Publishers
Egerton Ryerson Memorial Building
35 Britain Street,
Toronto M5A 1R7, Ontario

Printed and bound in Canada

Credits

Excerpts from *Mapping the Frontier: Charles Wilson's Diary of the Survey of the 49th Parallel, 1858-1862* edited by George F.G. Stanley, reprinted by permission of the Macmillan Company of Canada Limited.

Excerpts from *In Rupert's Land: Memoirs of Walter Traill* edited by Mae Atwood, reprinted by permission of McClelland and Stewart Limited, Toronto.

Glenbow-Alberta Institute: frontispiece, 13, 18, 43, 99, 100, 101, 119, 126, 127, 134

National Photography Collection, Public Archives of Canada: 3 (C-4572), 7 (C-79651), 9 (C-79636), 10 (C-79638), 11 (C-16757), 15 (C-79643), 19 (C-79639), 23 (C-17518), 27 (C-1732), 29 (C-81676), 31 (PA-74680), 33 (C-79640), 36 (PA-74666), 37 (C-7620), 39 (PA-9174), 42 (PA-51598), 47 (PA-74645), 51 (PA-74659), 53 (C-16447), 55 (PA-57923), 57 (PA-74652), 58 (PA-117931), 59 (PA-79735), 61 (PA-117819), 63 (PA-117818), 65 (PA-9170), 68 (C-5181), 75 (PA-9148), 77 (PA-7476), 79 (PA-9173), 81 (C-7376), 83 (PA-9169), 84 (PA-117816), 85 (PA-117815), 86 (PA-117817), 89 (C-78968), 92 (C-7879), 94 (C-88899), 97 (C-34943), 107 (C-88895), 116 (C-79001), 121 (PA-9133), 139 (C-88877), 139 (C-88876), 141 (C-37850), 146 (C-88878)

Geological Survey of Canada, National Photography Collection, Public Archives of Canada: 5 (C-7960), 17 (PA-39936), 35 (C-33881), 40 (C-1170), 41 (C-652), 44 (PA-39940)

Manitoba Archives: 21, 25, 49, 67, 69, 73

RCMP Museum, Regina, Saskatchewan: 70, 71

Beinecke Rare Book and Manuscript Library, Yale University: 91, 95, 96

Notman Photographic Archives: 93, 103, 105, 108, 122, 130, 149

Provincial Archives, Victoria, B.C.: 104, 109, 111, 112, 113, 115, 123, 125, 129, 133, 135, 137, 138, 140, 142, 143, 145, 147, 150

The Institution of Royal Engineers, Chatham, England: 117

American Museum of Natural History: 151, 152, 153, 155, 157, 159, 160, 161, 163, 164

Contents

Acknowledgements

This book, as with all publications containing historical material, is totally dependent upon the painstaking work of a long tradition of archivists. To all of these men and women I offer my most sincere thanks, for without their knowledge, experience and patience I would have been lost. I would like to acknowledge the assistance given me by Richard Huyda and Andrew Birrell of the National Photography Collection; apart from guiding me through the complexities of the collections, their excellent research on Hime, Baltzly and Horetzky has considerably eased my task. Stanley Triggs of the Notman Photographic Archives deserves a heartfelt thanks for his ever sage advice and superb photographs.

I cannot properly thank all of the friends and associates who have provided support and inspiration throughout the formation of this book, but be assured that your contributions have not been forgotten. Jon Whyte must be commended for sharing his literary skill and proofreading abilities. I thank Margery McDougall for her invaluable research assistance and Joan Schwartz for her enthusiasm and sharing of her knowledge of Frederick Dally.

I am deeply indebted to Mark Czarnecki and Evelyn Ross for their untold labours on and contributions to this book.

The research for this publication was kindly supported by the Canada Council Explorations Program.

E.C.

Dedicated to Robert Alexander

Introduction

Assiniboia, New Caledonia, Rupert's Land — magical names which still conjure up the image of a vast, cold, savage wilderness populated only by "red men" and halfbreed traders — these were the names of the Canadian West when it was the private preserve of the Hudson's Bay Company. From its inception in 1670, "The Company" enjoyed nearly two centuries of supremacy over an area two-thirds the size of Europe, a tract of land which was intentionally portrayed as a bastard child of the British Empire fit only to supply furs to the fashion houses of Europe. But in the 1850's the pressures of an ever-expanding world caused more attention to be paid to this sheltered land. The Americans were rapidly settling their West and threatening the British possessions to the north. The British, still smarting from the loss of the Oregon Territory by the Treaty of Washington in 1846, no longer accepted the assertion of Sir George Simpson, the Governor of the Company, that the West was unfit for habitation. The Canadians were also harbouring expansionist ideas — Confederation was in the wind and it was logical to assume that the eastern section of British North America would eventually gain control over the western portion, especially once the economically and politically essential "all British route" to the Pacific was established.

In 1857 the British dispatched an expedition under John Palliser to explore all aspects of the new land. That same year the Canadian Government sent out Henry Youle Hind with the Assiniboine and Saskatchewan Exploring Expedition to investigate the area in the vicinity of the Red River and to establish a route west from the Lakehead through Company territory. Between 1857 and 1885 the Canadian West teetered on the brink of "civilization". The forces of change arrived from two different directions and for quite different reasons. Some men came to the plains in search of settlement possibilities, sporting adventure and a route to the West, while those who arrived on the Pacific Coast went in search of gold or more mercantile sources of wealth.

British Columbia was the first area in the West to be blessed with civilization. In the spring of 1858, in response to the discovery of gold on the Fraser River, ten thousand gold seekers descended upon the tiny village of Victoria. Agricultural settlement was minimal, much to the chagrin of the more permanent citizens, and prospective settlers tended to be drawn off to the United States. The majority of the population of the colonies were American citizens, a fact which caused the nervous colonial government to mark the boundary to stave off a possible repeat of the lamentable Treaty of Washington. Between 1858 and 1862 the Royal Engineers marked the forty-ninth parallel from the coast to the Great Divide. The pursuit of gold led the prospectors up the Fraser and Thompson and further into the Interior. In 1861 a major gold discovery was made in the Cariboo region, and by 1864 the Royal Engineers had completed a wagon road through the Fraser Canyon to the new gold towns of Richfield and Barkerville. Small towns and road houses quickly sprang up along this route.

The colonies of British Columbia and Vancouver Island were united in 1866 and entered Confederation in 1871. By the 1870's most of the mining was being done by large companies; the rush was over and the boom towns of the Interior had subsided. British Columbia waited to see what the promised railroad would bring.

Meanwhile there had been a lull in official activities on the plains after the initial explorations by Palliser and Hind. During the 1860's the American Civil War and the difficulties involved in transferring lands from the Hudson's Bay Company to the Canadian Government inhibited development. The plains were left to the native population, gentlemen travellers, missionaries and the occasional prospector, all of whom were totally dependent upon the good graces of the Company for survival. By the end of the 1860's, anxiety over the land transfer and the presence of certain vociferous Canadians in the Red River Settlements led to the Métis Rebellion. The new Canadian Government sent in troops over the tedious Dawson Route from the Lakehead to quell what turned out to be an almost non-existent revolt.

The 1870's was a period of tremendous activity. Manitoba became a province, albeit a tiny one, in 1870. Between 1872 and 1874, partially to counteract the renewed interest of the Americans, the International Boundary was marked by the Royal Engineers from the Lake of the Woods to the Rocky Mountains. In 1874 the newly created North West Mounted Police arrived to maintain law and order in the wilderness. Throughout the 1870's survey parties under the direction of Sandford Fleming travelled the West in search of a route for the proposed transcontinental railroad. At the same time the Geological Survey of Canada set out to compile an inventory of natural resources.

The late 1870's and early 1880's saw small settlements appearing on the prairies. A flood of immigration was expected but would not come until the railroad was completed and the more actively promoted land in the United States was filled. In 1885 the rapid approach of European civilization, symbolized by the railroad, caused the Métis and some of the Indian tribes to attempt once again to establish their rights to a land rapidly becoming alien to them. This time the might of the Empire arrived by rail: the Métis nation was basically destroyed, and the West became the undisputed property of the "civilizers".

Many of the men who experienced the West during this transitional period committed their adventures in (and theories about) the new land to print. There were books by explorers, contradictory tomes on resource and agricultural possibilities by scholars, pamphlets by boosters and discourses by everyone on the proposed route of the railway, all intended to fill the evening hours of an eager public. Engravings enhanced books and the illustrated press: the words "from a photograph" ensured absolute authenticity. The public no longer depended on the romantic vision of painters who portrayed the wilderness according to the whims of artistic licence; photographs were real, and "from a photograph" was close enough.

The authors were as varied a group of characters as could be found anywhere, but diverse though their purposes and approaches were, the men who travelled the West shared a common British imperial attitude. From lowly Company clerk to English lord they shouldered the "white man's burden" with equal zeal. An absolute belief in the truth and rectitude of Christian, English civilization permitted the Victorian traveller to indulge in sweeping value judgements based upon the most superficial observations. The land was fallow and obviously should be made productive. The natives were savages and had to be civilized and Christianized. The way was simple and it was the British way.

William Francis Butler, a British Army officer unable to purchase his advancement, rushed from England to take part in the only action in the entire Empire, the expedition to deal with the 1870 Rebellion. *The Great Lone Land*, Butler's account of his journey through the West, shows him to be unique among his contemporaries: in the tradition of Cooper and Longfellow, he had a deep respect for and a romantic fascination with the native peoples. *The North-west Passage by Land* by Viscount Milton and Dr. Walter Cheadle became one of England's most popular travel books. These two young men were the first trans-Canadian tourists. Crossing the plains in 1862-63, they picked up the first Cana-

dian hitchhiker, the ludicrous Mr. O'Byrne, and proceeded to hack their way through the forests of British Columbia, travelling as little as a mile a day and guided by a Métis who had never crossed the Rockies. The book went through nine printings and became a Bible to those who followed them. The Earl of Southesk read and commented on a vast library of literature from *Romeo and Juliet* to *Chamber's Journal* as he hunted his way to and through the Rockies, shooting and eating nearly everything that moved: "I had a hind leg of the skunk for breakfast. It tasted like suckling pig; very white, soft and fat, but there was a suspicion of skunkiness about it that prevented me from finishing the plateful."

Along with the travellers and explorers came a new phenomenon, the photographer, hauling an appalling load of equipment (about 500 pounds) through the wilderness to capture for the civilized world images of the new land and its people. Cast in the same imperial mould, the photographers tended to substantiate the observations and attitudes of the writers.

Photography was in its infancy during this period. Prior to the introduction of the collodion wet-plate process in 1851, Daguerrian photography had been limited to studio portrait work. The wet-plate process yielded a clear, sharp negative from which many prints could be made, making field use practical. In 1858 in the Red River area, Humphrey Lloyd Hime was the first to use the new process successfully during a North American expedition. The process was very cumbersome, the photographer being obliged to carry his darkroom with him; the plate had to be coated, sensitized, exposed and developed on the spot. Each photograph could require from three to six hours of intense labour to produce, and the photographers encountered frustrating difficulties such as a lack of clean water and insects on the plates. Frederick Dally, while photographing in the interior of British Columbia, encountered a rattlesnake which insisted on licking the emulsion off a plate left to dry in the sun. Throughout the 1850's and 1860's the process was improved and exposure times decreased. In the 1870's a dry plate was introduced, eliminating the need for the dark tent, but exposures continued to be measured in seconds through minutes. Every scene had to be carefully considered, composed and structured to prevent movement.

When we view and judge these old photographs we must consider the eccentricities of the photographic process: what the photographer failed to record is almost as important as the images captured. The buffalo and the excitement of the chase had vanished by the time photography was capable of recording them. Dances, hailstorms, laughter, running the rapids, events at night or on a windy day — anything spontaneous or moving could not be recorded. The images left to us reflect the personal biases of the photographers, the limitations of the process and the demands of the customer, or, as in the case of survey photographers like Benjamin Baltzly and Charles Horetzky, the employer.

The itinerant commercial photographers were kept from the prairie regions by the difficulty of access and/or lack of clientele. A very few did visit the Red River in the 1860's, and in the late 1870's at least two men, W.E. Hook and George Anderton, photographed professionally on the plains. Commercial photographers arrived with the first wave of gold seekers to British Columbia, and their ranks swelled as the lucrative market expanded. One of the first to travel into the Interior was Charles Gentile, who accompanied Lieutenant Governor Seymour on his tour of the gold regions in 1865. It was customary at that time for photographers to purchase other photographers' plates and sell the prints as their own, hence it is often impossible to separate the work of Gentile, Dally, Richard Maynard and many others, all of whom took credit for the same pictures at various times.

Fascinated by early western Canadian photography and intrigued by the experiences and attitudes of the West's photographers, travellers and explorers, I began to form this book. Its contents represent only a miniscule portion of the material available. In my selection and editing I have chosen the strongest, most intriguing prose and images to reflect both the life style and attitudes most common in the period. The authors' attitudes are typical of the times; they are not my own. A general geographical ordering has shaped the book, but liberties have been taken with the placement and juxtaposition of texts and images to facilitate continuity. Because of the fluctuation of provincial and territorial boundaries, the present provincial boundaries have been used in identifying the photographs. Some of the photographs made by the Royal Engineers on the International Boundary Surveys were taken in the United States, but since this work was performed in a Canadian and British context it has been included as well.

The demise of the Hudson's Bay Company as autocratic ruler, the arrival of the North West Mounted Police, the North-west Rebellions and the construction of the Canadian Pacific Railway are significant historical events, but here they are only mentioned in passing. *Journeys to the Far West* is neither an illustrated history of Canada's West nor is it a history of the use and development of photography. It is a collage of thoughts, perceptions, observations, and photographs from a retreating past which I hope may lead to a better understanding of the people and the times in which those significant events occurred.

Edward Cavell
Banff
June 1979

Bibliography

Anderson, Samuel. *The North American Boundary from the Lake of the Woods to the Rocky Mountains.* London: Royal Geographical Society, 1876.

Atwood, Mae, editor. *In Rupert's Land: Memoirs of Walter Traill.* Toronto: McClelland and Stewart, 1970.

Ballantyne, Robert Michael. *Hudson Bay.* London: Thomas Nelson and Sons, 1879.

Butler, William Francis. *Far Out: Rovings Retold.* London: Wm. Isbister, 1880.

——————————. *The Great Lone Land.* London: Sampson Low, Marston, Searle and Rivington, 1879.

——————————. *The Wild North Land.* London: Sampson Low, Marston, Searle and Rivington, 1878.

Cheadle, Walter B. *Cheadle's Journal of a Trip Across Canada, 1862-1863.* Rutland, Vermont: Charles E. Tuttle and Company, Publishers, n.d.

Clark, Simon John. *"Diary of N.W.M.P. Experiences in N.W.T."* Unpublished manuscript, Glenbow-Alberta Institute.

D'Artigue, Jean. *Six Years in the Canadian North-West.* Toronto: Hunter, Rose and Co., 1882.

Gordon, Daniel M. *Mountain and Prairie.* Montreal: Dawson Brothers, 1880.

Graham, Frederick Ulric. *Notes of a Sporting Expedition in the Far West of Canada, 1847.* London: Private printing, 1898.

Grant, George M. *Ocean to Ocean.* Toronto: James Campbell and Son, 1873.

Hamilton, J.C. *The Prairie Province.* Toronto: Belford Brothers, 1876.

Hanington, C.F. *Journal from Quesnel through the Rocky Mountains during the winter of 1874-75,* Report on Canadian Archives, Ottawa, 1888.

Hind, Henry Youle. *Narrative of the Canadian Red River Exploring Expedition of 1857 and of the Assiniboine and Saskatchewan Exploring Expedition of 1858.* Two Volumes. London: Longman, Green, Longman and Roberts, 1860.

Horetzky, Charles. *Canada on the Pacific.* Montreal: Dawson Brothers, 1874.

Kane, Paul. *Wanderings of an Artist among the Indians of North America.* London: Longman, Green, Longman and Roberts, 1859.

Lord, John Keast. *The Naturalist in Vancouver Island and British Columbia.* Two Volumes. London: Richard Bentley, 1866.

——————————,("the Wanderer"). *At Home in the Wilderness.* London: Robert Hardwicke, 1867.

MacDonald, Duncan George Forbes. *British Columbia and Vancouver Island.* London: Longman, Green, Longman and Roberts, 1862.

Macfie, Matthew. *Vancouver Island and British Columbia.* London: Longman, Green, Longman and Roberts, 1865.

Mayne, R.C. *Four Years in British Columbia and Vancouver Island.* London: John Murray, 1862.

Messiter, Charles Alston. *Sport and Adventures Among the North American Indians.* London: R.H. Porter, 1890.

Milton, Viscount and Cheadle, W.B. *The North-west Passage by Land.* London: Cassell, Petter, and Galpin, 1866.

Musgrave, Anthony. *"Letter to the Earl of Granville, 1870."* Unpublished manuscript, Public Archives of Canada.

Palliser, John. *The Detailed Reports and Observations....* London: Queen's Printers, 1863.

Poole, Francis. *Queen Charlotte Islands.* London: Hurst and Blackett, 1872.

Simpson, Sir George. *Narrative of a Journey Around the World, 1841-42.* London: Henry Colburn, 1847.

Southesk, Earl of. *Saskatchewan and the Rocky Mountains.* Edinburgh: Edmonston and Douglas, 1875.

Stanley, George F.G., editor. *Mapping the Frontier: Charles Wilson's Diary of the Survey of the 49th Parallel, 1858-1862.* Toronto: Macmillan of Canada, 1970.

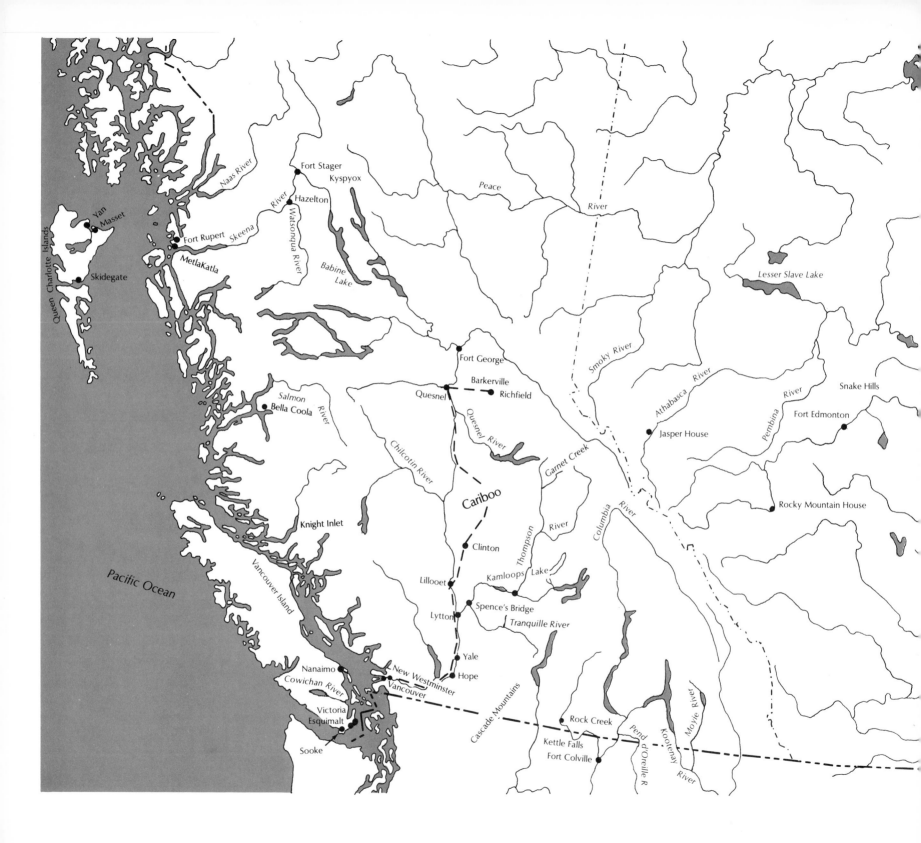

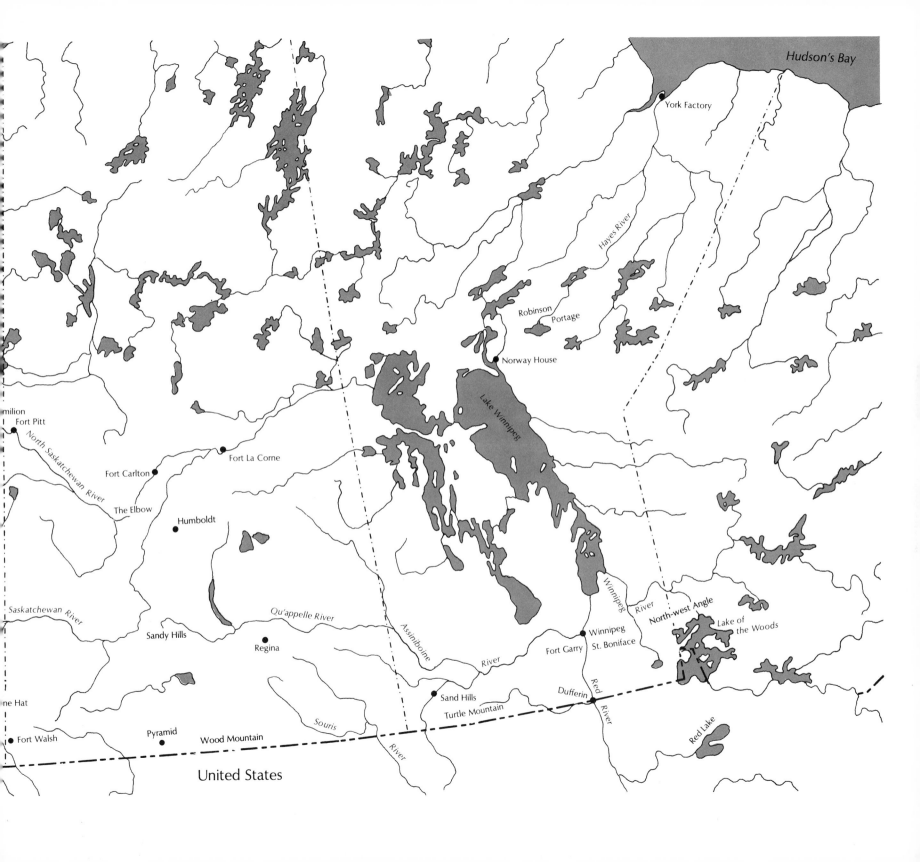

Hudson's Bay

York Factory

Hayes River

Robinson
Portage

Norway House

Lake Winnipeg

milion
Fort Pitt

North Saskatchewan River

Fort Carlton

Fort La Corne

The Elbow

Humboldt

Saskatchewan River

Qu'appelle River

Sandy Hills

Regina

Winnipeg
St. Boniface

Fort Garry

Winnipeg River

North-west Angle

Lake of
the Woods

Assiniboine

River

ne Hat

Sand Hills

Dufferin

Red River

Turtle Mountain

Souris

Fort Walsh

Pyramid

Wood Mountain

River

Red Lake

United States

Photographers' camp, North American Boundary Commission, 1873. Photo by: Royal Engineers

PART 1

MANITOBA

Breaking Camp

The dawn of morning and the early start in this rocky wilderness possess some characteristics peculiar to the country and the strange companions with whom necessity compels you to associate. Rising from a bed on the hard rock, which you have softened by a couple of rugs or a north blanket, and if time and opportunity permitted by fresh spruce or pine boughs, the aspect of the sky first claims and almost invariably receives attention. The morning is probably calm, the stars are slightly paling, cold yellow light begins to show itself in the east; on the river or lake rests a screen of dense fog, landwards a wall of forest impenetrable to the eye. Walking a step or two from the camp a sudden rush through the underbrush tells of a fox, mink, or marten prowling close by, probably attracted by the remains of last night's meal. From the dying campfires a thin column of smoke rises high above the trees, or spreads lakewards to join the damp misty veil which hides the quiet waters from view. Around the fires are silent forms like shrouded corpses stretched at full length on the bare rock or on spruce branches carefully arranged. These are the Indians; they have completely enveloped themselves in their blankets, and lie motionless on their backs. Beneath upturned canoes, or lying like the Indians with their feet to the fire, the French voyageurs are found scattered about the camp; generally the servant attached to each tent stretches himself before the canvas door. No sound at this season of the year disturbs the silence of the early dawn if the night has been cold and calm. The dull music of a distant waterfall is sometimes heard, or its unceasing roar when camped close to it as on the Rattlesnake Portage, but these are exceptional cases; in general all Nature seems sunk in perfect repose, and the silence is almost oppressive. As the dawn advances an Indian awakes, uncovers his face, sits on his haunches and looks around from beneath the folds of his blanket which he has drawn over his head. After a few minutes have thus passed, not observing his companions show any sign of waking or disposition to rise, he utters a low "waugh"; slowly other forms unroll themselves, sit on their haunches and look around in silence. Three or four minutes are allowed to pass away when one of them rises and arranges the fire, adding fresh wood and blowing the embers into a flame. He calls a French voyageur by name, who leaps from his couch and in a low voice utters, "Lève, lève." Two or three of his companions quickly rise, remain for a few minutes on their knees in prayer, and then shout lustily, "Lève, messieurs, lève." In another minute all is life, the motionless forms under the canoes, by the campfires, under trees, or stretched before the tent doors spring to their feet. The canvas is shaken and ten minutes given to dress, the tent pins are then unloosened and the half-dressed laggard rushes into the open air to escape the damp folds of the tent now threatening to envelop him. Meanwhile the canoes are launched and the baggage stowed away. The voyageurs and travellers take their seats, a hasty look is thrown around to see that no stray frying pan or hatchet is left behind, and the start is made. An effort to be cheerful and sprightly is soon damped by the mist into which we plunge, and no sound but the measured stroke of the paddle greets the ear. The sun begins to glimmer above the horizon, the fog clears slowly away, a loon or a flock of ducks fly wildly across the bow of the first canoe, the Indians and voyageurs shout at the frightened birds or imitate their cry with admirable accuracy, the guide stops, pipes are lit, and a cheerful day is begun.

Henry Youle Hind

PART 1
MANITOBA

Assiniboine and Saskatchewan Exploring Expedition, camp by the Red River, Manitoba, 1858. Photo by: Humphrey Lloyd Hime

Lunch

At eleven o'clock we reached Island Portage, having paddled thirty-two miles — the best forenoon's work since taking to the canoes — in spite of the weather. Here a stream launch is stationed; and, though the engineer thought it a frightful day to travel in, he got ready at our request, but said that he could not go four miles an hour as the rain would keep the boiler wet the whole time. We dined with M —— 's party under the shelter of their upturned canoe on tea and the fattest of fat pork, which all ate with delight unspeakable, for there was the right kind of sauce. The day and our soaked condition suggested a little brandy as a specific; but their bottle was exhausted and, an hour before, they had passed round the cork for each to have a "smell" at, in lieu of a "drain."...The Indians excited our admiration: soaked through and overworked as they had been, the only word that we heard indicating that they were conscious of anything unusual was an exclamation from Baptiste as he gave himself a shake, "Boys, wish I was in a tavern now, I'd get drunk in less than t'ree hours, I guess."

George Grant

Mosquitoes

They assail every inch of the body. By day they bite through the socks, by night through the sheets, or they settle upon the nose and forehead, and woe betide the sleeper who has a rent in his curtains. These buzzing insects have actually brought horses and cattle to a painful and lingering death. So great is the misery which these pests entail upon the human race that whole families have been forced to leave their homes for months together.

"I believe," says a gentleman writing from Norway, "there is no preventative against their bite, which is instantaneous. They dash through the smoke of strong tobacco like a foxhound through a bullfinch; they creep under veil or gloves like a ferret into a rabbit-hole; where they can neither dash nor creep, they bide their own time with the pertinacious cunning of a Red Indian. Wherever the clothes touch the body closely, at the knees and elbows, they swarm in thousands and bite through and through; they creep in single file up the seams of gloves and try each stitch in succession. I have seen my friend's coat and hat so covered, as he walked in front, that I could at any time kill the shape of my hand in mosquitoes at a blow; and I have seen the unhappy horses so overlaid from ears to tail with a clustering mass of wings that with the point of my finger, placed anywhere, I could crush several of the bloodthirsty little demons. One question always puzzled me: what do they live on when they don't meet travellers?"

Duncan MacDonald

Repairs

The Indians never halt without at once turning their canoes upside down and examining them. The seams and crevices in the birch bark yield at any extra strain, and scratches are made by submerged brushwood in some of the channels or the shallow parts of the lakes. These crevices they carefully daub over with resin, which is obtained from the red pine, till the bottom of an old canoe becomes almost covered with a black resinous coat.

George Grant

Hauling a York boat over the Robinson Portage, Manitoba, 1878. Photo by: Dr. Robert Bell

Hailstorm

In descending this branch of the Winnipeg, a terrific thunderstorm accompanied by a hurricane of wind and an extraordinary fall of hailstones approached us from the south as we reached the high portage which connects this route with the great river. Turning round in my canoe I saw, about half a mile in our rear, a white line of foam advancing rapidly towards us. Directing the attention of Lambert, who occupied the stern to the approaching squall, he instantly changed the course of the canoe to the opposite bank. The river here was about 300 yards broad and we were swiftly paddling close to the west side, which was bounded by high and precipitous granite rocks. I had barely time to stretch a gutta-percha cloth over the canoe before the hurricane came down upon us. Lying, as directed, at full length on the floor of our small craft, I left her to the dexterity of Lambert and the Indian. They met the shock skilfully and paddled before the storm with great rapidity, as did also our fellow travellers in the other canoe. We continued on our way for some minutes, gradually drawing near to the right bank where we intended to land. Suddenly, however, large hailstones began to descend with such force as to bruise my hands severely in endeavouring to retain the covering in its place. The Indian in the bow laughed heartily at first, but having no covering on his head beyond his thick and matted hair, he soon crouched and drew a part of the gutta-percha cloth over him. Lambert being provided with a thick fur cap held bravely on, although he loudly exclaimed that the hailstones were bruising his hands and he would not be able to paddle much longer. Fortunately we were now close to the bank, and Lambert called out to the Indian to keep the canoe from striking against the rocks. A few strokes of the paddles brought us within a yard of the shore when the Indian, lightly springing out of the canoe, caught her bow as she was about to strike the rock. I succeeded in disentangling myself from the covering, which was pressed down by an accumulation of hailstones enough to have filled at least three buckets.

Henry Youle Hind

Barter

In his canoe we found his wife and two children. The half-naked little savages were busily engaged in plucking a goose for their noon-day meal. I offered him some tea in exchange for the bird and, when the transfer was made, asked him what they intended to eat for their own dinner; he replied by pointing to the bow of his canoe, addressing at the same time a word or two to his wife, who raised a piece of birch bark and disclosed two more geese which he had shot a few minutes before we saw him. Having bartered for them also with a small plug of tobacco, I asked the guide what he would take for a new stone pipe which one of the children was playing with; to my astonishment the Indian replied three beaver skins (about five shillings), but at the same time casting his eyes upon our cups and saucers which lay on the grass, he said he would prefer a cup, worth about four pence. He really knew nothing of the value of money or of cups, although he was quite aware of the worth of a beaver skin in ordinary articles of trade such as powder, shot, tobacco, or tin-ware, but a painted earthenware cup was something new to him; and his wife expressed great delight as she examined with much minuteness the addition to her household goods.

Henry Youle Hind

Delayed

We had not punted more than two hours and a half when we found the canoe leaking and were obliged to put ashore at an old deserted hunting camp on the left bank of the river. We then discovered that the women had not been able to resist the temptation of eating the grease instead of mixing it with the gum, so it all cracked off again and we had to occupy ourselves with staunching our canoe for the rest of the evening.

John Palliser

Indian camp, North-west Angle, Lake of the Woods, Ontario, 1872. Photo by: Royal Engineers

Ill Repute

Never at any time since first the white man was welcomed on the newly-discovered shores of the western continent by his red brother, never has such disaster and destruction overtaken these poor, wild, wandering sons of Nature as at the moment in which we write. Of yore it was the pioneers of France, England, and Spain with whom they had to contend, but now the whole white world is leagued in bitter strife against the Indian. The American and Canadian are only names that hide beneath them the greed of united Europe. Terrible deeds have been wrought out in that western land; terrible heart-sickening deeds of cruelty and rapacious infamy — have been, I say? no, are to this day and hour, and never perhaps more sickening than now in the full blaze of nineteenth-century civilization. If on the long line of the American frontier, from the Gulf of Mexico to the British boundary, a single life is taken by an Indian, if even a horse or ox be stolen from a settler, the fact is chronicled in scores of journals throughout the United States, but the reverse of the story we never know. The countless deeds of perfidious robbery, of ruthless murder done by white savages out in these western wilds never find the light of day. The poor red man has no telegraph, no newspaper, no type, to tell his sufferings and his woes.

William Francis Butler

Peace Treaty

The Indians said, "A year ago these people (the Company) drew lines and measured and marked the land as their own — why was this? We own the land, the Manitou gave it to us. There was no bargain; they stole from us and now they steal from you. When they were small the Indians treated them with love and kindness; now there is no withstanding them, they are first in everything." Governor Morris asked, "Who made all men? — the Manitou. It is not stealing to make use of His gifts." The Indian Pah-tah-kay-we-nin replied thus beautifully, "True, even I, a child, know that God gives us land in different places, and when we meet together as friends, we ask from each other and do not quarrel as we do so." Says the narrator, "State policy *not* philanthropy, and that briefly, will effect philanthropy's noblest work — the teeming and hardly-used peoples of the Old World will here find a home, their moiety and fee — even as their life — so plain that in the beautiful words of Pah-tah-kay-we-nin, 'Even I who am a little child know that.' It was done, a little crowding — the low-toned voices and laughter of the Indians, a touch of the pen and an empire changed hands!"

J.C. Hamilton

Chippewa Indians at Dufferin, Manitoba, 1873-74. Photo by: Royal Engineers

9

Chippewa Indians near Dufferin, Manitoba, 1873. Photo by: Royal Engineers

On the bank at the crossing-place the skeletons of Indian wig-wams and sweating-houses were grouped in a prominent position, just above a fishing weir where the Ojibways of this region take large quantities of fish in the spring. The framework of a large medicine wigwam measured twenty-five feet in length by fifteen in breadth; the sweating-houses were large enough to hold one man in a sitting position, and differed in no respect from those frequently seen on the canoe route between Lakes Superior and Winnipeg, and which have been often described by travellers.

Henry Youle Hind

Steamer landing, North-west Angle, Lake of the Woods, Ontario, 1872 (McPherson home in background). Photo by: Royal Engineers

Home Free

I should like to know who is able to boast a more perfect independence than is he who has learned the art, for art it most assuredly is, of being "at home in the wilderness." What cares such a one for quarter-day; no flinty-hearted landlord threatens to sell him up if the rent is not paid; that terrible man, the tax gatherer, has no terrors for him and never "just looks in" with his ugly book and an ink bottle dangling from the coat button for his little account, which it is not at all times convenient to pay. All the collectors that ever were, or ever will be, could not in the wilderness cut off your water supply or stop your light. I quite agree in opinion with that dweller in the wilds who, when the newly-arrived settler boasted that the sun never set upon England's possessions, naively replied, "Wa'al stranger, that ar likely enough, kase 'tis low'd by all as cum from thim parts that the tax bos never camps down to sleep." At home in the wilderness in right good earnest you live rent free, pay no taxes, get fuel for the trouble of cutting it, and water and light without paying a rate; though surrounded with an abundance of fish, flesh, and fowl, you are free from meat bills, nothing to lock into your house, and no thieves to lock out; front door and latchkey are useless encumbrances; you wear what you like, do what you like, go out when you like, come home when you like, snap your fingers at "Mrs. Grundy," and care less for her evil tongue than the bite of a mosquito.

John Keast Lord

Bugs

This was another lovely day but, for all that, we rejoiced when a thunderstorm came on, for it drove away those pests — the venomous, eye-blinding, hard-skinned little sand flies. Yesterday another enemy had troubled us — certain huge-headed gadflies, of hornet appearance, that are commonly known as "bulldogs." Darting on man or horse, the wretch gives one short bite with his scissory clippers — then off like a flash, leaving a poisoned and bleeding wound.

The insect tribe is a perfect curse; one has no rest or peace. Mosquitoes on the wet ground and sand flies in the dry, bulldogs in the sunshine, bugs in the oak woods, ants everywhere — it is maddening.... The fever caused by these bites is what most distresses me. It is worst at night, when one gets warm in bed; all the veins swell and glow and seem full of liquid fire.

James Carnegie, Earl of Southesk

Rude Awakening

This report handed in, I started for Canada in horse-sleds over the snow. It was slow work, not more than twenty miles each day. I had as fellow travellers a gentleman and his secretary, who had been sent from the Colonial Office in London to Winnipeg to report upon matters there, and an archdeacon, on his way to England to collect funds for the Church Mission in the new province of Manitoba. We slept each night in the cabin of some Red River halfbreed settler, laying our blankets on the floor in a row, the archdeacon usually having the centre. One night the archdeacon sprang from his couch shouting, "They are putting guns through the window; they are going to fire!" A crash of breaking glass seemed to confirm his alarm. I caught at the supposed gun barrel. It was the tail of a cow. The animal had been rubbing the hind part of her person against the small window-frame, and her tail had broken the window and our sleep together.

William Francis Butler

Trader McPherson and family, North-west Angle, Lake of the Woods, Ontario, 1872. Photo by: Royal Engineers

Gunsmith

Putting up a piece of canvas considerably larger than a house door, Pierre withdrew some thirty paces and blazed away but without the slightest result. By no means discouraged, the persevering fellow immediately set to work to improve his gun. He filed and hammered at the barrel and twisted it about with his hands; finally he thrust a long stick down it, then placing the projecting end between the cartwheel spokes, levered with might and main till he thought the tube was sufficiently straight. Absurd as all this seemed, it really improved the gun which, being of the same pattern as those bought by the Indians and rendered serviceable by similar rough doctoring, was in time likely to become a fairly useful weapon, at any rate for extremely short ranges.

James Carnegie, Earl of Southesk

The Hunt

Milton and I start to run some fine white timber wolves which were hanging about. Milton has a good start on the one large white fellow. I some one-half mile behind. He gets close up to him on the Old Red and fires several balls at him without effect. I then come up on the little roan of Vital's which Milton lent me, my own horse having a galled back from the long journey of yesterday. I get close up and fire both barrels: miss. Little mare who had gone well completely done and I reluctantly give up the chase, the wolf being now able to run away from her. I strike out for the road and presently discern Milton in the distance. We canter along for seven or eight miles some time in the dark, at last see camp fire; arrive very cold and hungry and very cross. Milton blows up. Row with Messiter. Find he has killed two bulls and wounded another which he lost, having expended all his bullets. Milton and Messiter very angry with one another about nothing as usual. Quieten down.

Walter Cheadle

Sharpshooters

Those fellows were dressed in the unmistakable Hudson's Bay capot, and were each armed with an old flint gun, with which they rather astonished our botanist. A flock of grey geese happening to pass a short distance, Mr. Mac jokingly pointed to them and, by signs, signified his desire to see them shoot. The two aborigines, motioning to us to keep quiet, immediately began to imitate the cackling of geese, and looking up, we saw the flock swerve slightly in their course and turn in our direction. When within shooting distance, although to our unpractised eyes they were yet too far, *bang, bang* went the guns, and a couple of plump geese fell into the grass beside us. These were a welcome addition to our larder, and proved a wholesome and palatable change from pemmican. A plug of tobacco apiece in payment was received by the Indians with evident marks of pleasure, and they good-naturedly set to work to assist in collecting firewood and doing other little chores of the camp.

Charles Horetzky

14

Maxim Marion, Métis guide, 1872.
Photo by: Royal Engineers

Dog Teams

My team consists of three middle-sized Indian dogs, sharp-nosed, bushy-haired and wolfish. Chocolat, the leader, is dark red; Casse-toute, grey, shaded with black; and Fox, reddish-fawn colour. The driver is a particularly smart and active man; he can run for miles behind the cariole while the dogs are galloping, encouraging them all the time with incessant volleys of abuse in a mixture of English, French, and Indian.

(Vociferously) Fox! Fox! ah, crapaud Fox! (Screamingly) Faux! sacré démon! (Warningly) Fox, ye ould sinner, pren' garde: crapaud that ye aire. (Surprised) Chócolat! (Very distinctly and syllabically) Chóc-ó-lát — michástim! [Michastim, Michastemue — bad dog, bad dogs: the nearest approach to swearing, I am told, that the Indian language admits of.] — Yéu-oh! yéu-oh! [to the right]: — cha! cha! [the left]. (Parenthetically) Ah, Chocolat, you weell catch it presently. (Indignantly and suddenly) Casse-toute: ah, sal-au-prix! (Shriekingly) Casse-toute!! (Contemptuously) mauvais chien! (Despairingly — as if calling to a dog in the sky) Fox! Fox! Faux! Then a burst of unintelligible Indian rough words, followed by a hasty, furious shout to the whole team — Fox! Casse-toute! Chocolat! cré démons! — under cover of which he rushes past the cariole shaking his whip, while the wretched dogs dart from side to side in agonies of fear, whining, squealing, and shrieking like a drove of distracted pigs....

The cruelty with which dogs are treated here cannot be excused. Doubtless they are often obstinate and provoking and require severe floggings — especially from a new driver, till he has brought his team into subjection — but when one sees poor helpless animals who are undergoing extreme labour in the trains not merely beaten on the body with heavy lashes but systematically flogged on the head till their ears drip blood; and not merely this, but beaten with whip handles till their jaws and noses are cut open with deep wounds; and not merely this, but cudgelled with clubs, and knelt upon and stamped upon till their howls turn to low groans of agony — this I say is enough to call down vengeance on the land....

The strange thing is that men who are full of kindness and humanity towards one another and towards the rest of creation should be as bad as the greatest ruffians in their treatment of the poor dogs — those most useful slaves who will work day and night, almost without a rest, for weeks together. But for them there would be no means of travelling during the many months of snow, which no thaw removes till melted by the strengthened sun in April.

James Carnegie, Earl of Southesk

Courtesy

While breakfast was being prepared by one of us, the others gathered and packed our traps in bundles adapted to the carrying capabilities of each individual. Neither were our canine friends forgotten, for Sinclair prepared four diminutive loads of about fifteen or twenty pounds each with which we loaded each dog, which followed in our tracks with the gravity and decorum due to the occasion. It was amusing to watch the sagacious brutes when by any chance one or other of us lagged behind, as we sometimes did. One and all would then step aside and courteously give the precedence in order to benefit by the better beaten track.

Charles Horetzky

Sent to Rome

I witnessed the first example of a very common occurrence in dog driving — I beheld the operation known as "sending a dog to Rome." This consists simply of striking him over the head with a large stick until he falls perfectly senseless to the ground; after a little he revives and, with memory of the awful blows that took his consciousness away full upon him, he pulls frantically at his load. Oftentimes a dog is "sent to Rome" because he will not allow the driver to arrange some hitch in the harness; then, while he is insensible, the necessary alteration is carried out, and when the dog recovers he receives a terrible lash of the whip to set him going again. The halfbreeds are a race easily offended, prone to sulk if reproved; but at the risk of causing delay and inconvenience I had to interfere with a peremptory order that "sending to Rome" should be at once discontinued in my trains.

William Francis Butler

Landing white whales at York Factory, Manitoba, 1880. Photo by: Dr. Robert Bell

17

Cutting ice on the Red River, Manitoba, 1873. Photo by: Royal Engineers

It is amusing when camping in the snow to observe the little artifices put in practice to make your neighbour get up and renew the fire instead of doing it yourself. I have seen men pretend to have nightmares, screaming and kicking in furious style; then they have coughing fits or roll against their neighbour. Anything is better than getting up yourself, as it means wading through the snow to fetch more wood and sometimes going far into the timber to get it, and taking a good deal of snow into your bag when you turn in again.

Sleeping out in a snowstorm is a curious experience till you are used to it. Snow falls so rapidly in that country that you very soon have from six to eighteen inches of snow on you; and I shall never forget my feelings when, waking up one morning and putting my head out of my bag, I found myself, as I thought, deserted. The whole prairie for miles was perfectly level; the dogs, sleigh, and my companions were all gone, and it was most curious, when the real state of the case occurred to me and I had shouted several times, to see the snow open in one spot and reveal a man's head, and in another a dog's. On this occasion enough snow had fallen to cover the sleigh and everything on it, the latter being some fifteen inches high.

Charles Messiter

Surveyor East's party, North-west Angle, Lake of the Woods, Ontario, 1872. Photo by: Royal Engineers

Steamboat

Thursday, the tenth of June, was a notable day at Fort Garry. The first steamer that had yet navigated the Red River made her appearance that morning, bringing two or three passengers from Minnesota. *Ans Northup* was the name of this small, shabby, stern-wheel boat, mean and insignificant in itself but important as the harbinger of new developments of what Americans are pleased to call civilization.

Crowds of Indians stood silently on the shore watching the arrival of this strange portentous object. Little thought they how ominous a sight it was for them, fraught with presages of ruin for all their wandering race!

James Carnegie, Earl of Southesk

Civilization

To civilize a new land is the easiest of tasks if we but set about it after the American model. Here is the recipe. Given a realm from which the red man has been banished, tricked, shot, or hunted out; from which the bison and elk have been chased; a lonely, tenantless land, with some great river flowing in long winding reaches silently through its vast plains and mountain gorges: here, then, is what you have to do:

Place on the river a steamboat of the rudest construction. Wherever the banks are easy of ascent, or where a smaller stream seeks the main river, build a drinking-house of rough-hewn logs; let the name of God be used only in blasphemy, and language be a medium for the conveyance of curses. Call a hill a "bluff," a valley a "gulch," a firefly a "lightning bug," a man a "cuss," three shanties a "city." Let every man chew when he isn't smoking, and spit when he isn't asleep; and then — when half a dozen persons have come to violent ends — when killing has literally become "no murder" — your new land will be thoroughly civilized....

I know not how it is, but in wild glen or lonely prairie, amidst races whose very names are supposed to be synonymous with all that is wild, lawless, or barbarous, I have known many a bond of sympathy, many a link 'twixt their lives and mine own. Nay, when man has been far distant, and nought but the lone spaces lay around me, and the gaunt pine tree stretched its arms athwart the icy sky, I have felt companionship and friendship for the very dogs that drew my load; but for this band of civilizers, for these brutal pioneers of Anglo-American freedom, in their many stages between unblackened boots and diamond breastpins, I have felt nothing but loathing and disgust.

William Francis Butler

Fort Garry, Manitoba, 1873. Photo by: Royal Engineers

Faith

Soon after our arrival at the Red Lake mission we learned that the Roman Catholic missionary had been frozen to death two days previously in an attempt to cross the ice during a snowstorm from a promontory about two miles away from the mission. He had been visiting a camp of Ojibways, who warned him of the perils of a return across the ice during the storm, and invited him to pass the night in their wigwams; but the missionary thought that he would not incur any danger of freezing during so short a traverse, although the thermometer indicated a temperature of 25° below zero at the opposite station.

He was frozen within two hundred yards of the mission house, near to which were a number of log houses, tenanted at the time by halfbreeds and Indians. When the body was found on the following morning, a number of Indians set themselves to trace his steps from the Ojibway camp across the ice, a difficult undertaking, in consequence of the high wind which was blowing at the time having, to an inexperienced eye, obliterated all traces of his steps. With astonishing accuracy these wild men read the brief history of his journey, and related the incidents to me as we stood on the banks of Red Lake with the Ojibway village and the course of the unfortunate missionary in view. "There," said my dusky informant, pointing to the ice not more than half a mile from the houses, "there he first turned his back to the wind, and there he knelt to pray," the Indian suiting the action to the word, and kneeling in the attitude which the track showed the missionary had assumed. Now he faced the wind and ran against the blinding snow and pitiless storm; here he turned his back again; there his tracks showed how he slipped and fell, and once again where he knelt to pray. The marks of his fingers were seen on the crust of snow lying in frozen patches on the ice. Once more he fell, rose again, knelt for a while, and made a last effort to push against the storm. They came at length to where he had fallen for the last time, and subsequently knelt with his hands on the ice, his head touching the snow. He was found with hands clasped in the attitude of prayer, his head bent upon his breast. The barking dogs at the mission must have been aware that he was approaching, notwithstanding the gloom of evening and the drifting snow, for they bayed fiercely in the direction he was coming about the time he was supposed to have fallen. The halfbreeds heard the dogs and looked out in expectation of seeing the missionary approach, but as the dogs soon ceased to bark they thought it was a false alarm and did not go to meet and assist him.

It was painfully interesting to watch the Indians relate the narrative of this short but terrible journey from the information they had gathered on the almost trackless ice and snow. The imitation of the actions and motions of the poor missionary, his attitude of prayer, his drooping head touching the cold ice, his backward wanderings were all so faithfully represented, so true to nature, that the reality seemed to be occurring before me rather than the solemn mimicry of a savage.

After the Indian who was most active in impersonating the missionary had finished his mournful tale, he quietly took a lighted pipe from one of his companions standing by and, drawing his blanket over his head, seated himself upon the prostrate trunk of a tree, and without any expression of feeling covertly glanced in my face to see the effect of his narrative; and when I asked him through the halfbreed interpreter where the body was lying, he coldly pointed with one finger to a log hut close by, without withdrawing the pipe from his mouth or showing any further interest in the matter.

Henry Youle Hind

Roman Catholic cathedral and nunnery, St. Boniface, Manitoba, 1858. Photo by: Humphrey Lloyd Hime

John

On Sunday we attended service in Pratt's house; the Rev. Mr. Settee read the prayers in English with great ease and correctness; he preached in Ojibway, and a hymn was sung in the Cree language. Before the sermon the missionary surprised us by waking up a drowsy Indian who was enjoying a quiet nap in a corner of the room and, leading him to the temporary reading desk, commenced the ceremony of public baptism. My astonishment was not diminished when the reverend gentleman, turning to me without any preliminary notice, said abruptly, "Name this man!" After a moment's reflection I said "John," and without any unnecessary loss of time or words, "John" walked to his bench and was soon apparently lost, in noisy slumber, to all consciousness of the privileges and blessings of which adult Christian baptism, duly received, had made him the inheritor.

Henry Youle Hind

Sunday Best

The congregations at Red River consist of resident and retired officers of the Hudson's Bay Company, some merchants, farmers, and the natives or halfbreeds of the respective parishes. The services are conducted in strict accordance with customary forms, and the demeanour of the congregations is very attentive and decorous. A fair proportion of the congregations come to and go from church in neat carriages or on horseback, and the external appearance of the assemblages, taken as a whole, in relation to dress is superior to what we are accustomed to see in Canada or in the country parishes of Great Britain. The young men wear handsome blue cloth frock coats with brass buttons, and round their waist a long scarlet woollen sash; the young women are neatly dressed like the country girls at home, but in place of a bonnet they wear the far more becoming shawl or coloured handkerchief thrown over or tied round the head; sometimes they allow their long black hair to serve the purpose of a covering and ornament for which, from its profusion, it is admirably fitted. In this particular many of the halfbreed girls follow the custom of their Indian ancestry who, as a general rule, never cover the head.

Henry Youle Hind

Blasphemy

It is greatly to the credit of the Indians in British America that they have never injured or stolen from any missionary. They have plundered posts, stripped traders naked, and murdered some who perhaps had given them cause; but even when at war, the missionary is allowed to enter and speak in their great councils and is everywhere treated with respect. Reverence is a strong trait in the Indian character. His own language supplies no words for profane swearing; if he wishes to blaspheme, he must borrow from the French or English.

George Grant

Grace

Hardisty told us of contest between priest and Methodist minister, Mr. Wolsey. Priest catches a convert and baptises him. Wolsey hears of it and baptises him over again, and so on ad infinitum, it being with great difficulty that convert knows whether he was made Papist or Protestant last. Quarrelled very fiercely at table about saying grace at dinner when both staying at the fort. Mr. Brazeau who was in charge at the time told them if they did not behave better they should neither of them be allowed to say it at all. Whereupon they compromised and agreed to say it alternately. The priest did not understand English, and Wolsey not French. Priest tried Latin; Wolsey at fault. They were therefore driven to Cree of which they neither knew much. Their "Keya Margastun, niya mirvarsin," "keya a rascal," "keya crapeau" intensely amused Brazeau and Macaulay who were the spectators.

Walter Cheadle

Missionary and Indian, c.1870.
Photo by: Ryder Larsen

The Dance

After we had discussed some meat, cakes, pasties, tea, and whisky spread out on the ground outside, we adjourned to the ballroom, the sitting room of the little two-roomed house. It was crowded with guests dressed in full halfbreed finery. At one end were two fiddlers who worked in relays, the music being in most rapid time and doubtless very fatiguing to the instrumentalists. The dance, in which about half a dozen couples were engaged when we entered, appeared to be a kind of cross between a Scotch reel and the "Lancers," a number of lively steps, including a double-shuffle and stamp, being executed with great vigour. The dancing was dancing and no mistake, and both the men and their fair partners were exceedingly hot and exhausted when the "set" was finished. The figures appeared so intricate, and the skill of the performers so admirable, that we were deterred by our natural diffidence from yielding to the repeated solicitations of the M.C. to select partners and foot it with the rest. At length, however, Milton, with a courage equal to the occasion and, it is suspected, strongly attracted by the beauty of the bride — a delicate-featured, pensive-looking girl of sixteen or seventeen, with a light and graceful figure — boldly advanced and led her out amid the applause of the company. He succeeded in interpreting the spirit of the music, if not with the energy certainly with a greater dignity and infinitely less exertion than his compeers. His performance was highly appreciated by all — including Treemiss and Cheadle — who gazed with admiration, mingled with envy, at a success they were unequal to achieve.

Milton and Cheadle

Betrothal

I saw the Indian chief coming towards me, leading by the hand the young Uskinik squaw, my dancing partner of the previous night, and followed by the councillor and the petty chiefs. Of course I was somewhat curious to know what could be the object of this early morning visit; and to my sorrow, I soon learned what it was. Without uttering a word, the Indians walked into the wigwam and sat down. Then the chief took out a pipe and, smoking a few minutes, passed it to another who followed his example, and so on, till all had smoked the pipe of peace. This done, the councillor arose and began to speak with remarkable vehemence and volubility. I could understand nothing of what he said but "Uskinik squaw," which he often repeated, pointing at the same time towards the young girl. But from the countenance of my host, which grew more and more gloomy as the speaker went on, and from his occasional glances at me, I could understand that this discourse foreboded me no good. When the councillor had ceased to speak, my host told me that the chief, as a proof and pledge of his pacific sentiments towards the whites, had resolved to give his daughter to the white man whom he considered most worthy of that honour, and that it was upon me his choice had fallen, and he now brought her to me, hoping I would fully appreciate the honour he wished to confer upon me. Honour indeed! I was terrified. My first reflections were regrets that I had been foolish enough to venture among the Indians alone and then, how to safely get rid of that honour. To refuse would bring upon me imprisonment and torture, perhaps death. To marry, and desert her, I would not. To marry and live with her would be worse than death. What was I to do? I could see no way out of my difficulty but to appear to acquiesce, that I might gain time to get away from them. So, resolving upon this course, I charged my host to say to the chief that, being neither a great warrior nor a mighty hunter, I was far from expecting so great an honour; but, if he absolutely insisted on having me for his son-in-law, I begged for a delay of a few days in order to give my friends at Edmonton time to come and witness the wedding, adding that it was the custom among the whites to invite many guests and to make great preparations for such an important event. My answer not only seemed to satisfy but to greatly please the old chief; and, considering the affair settled, he arose, and with his followers retired. Congratulating myself on having escaped from such a dilemma, and for having succeeded in gaining the above respite, I felt sure of escaping them altogether.

Jean d'Artigue

Laetitia Bird, a Cree halfbreed, Red River Settlements, Manitoba, 1858. Photo by: Humphrey Lloyd Hime

Forts

The name "fort" applied to these posts of the H.B. Company is frequently imposing in more ways than one. It naturally suggests walls, bastions, loopholes, formidable gateways, a fortified residence, palisades, etc; but frequently...the reality is very different from the vision. A small single-storied dwelling made of hewn logs little better than the rude farmhouse of a Canadian backwoodsman, a trading store as plain as the dwelling, a smoke-house for curing and storing fish and meat, and a stable constitute the whole establishment.

Rev. Daniel Gordon

Making Do

I asked Ta-wa-pit what he would do for a smoke until he had finished the new pipe. After the halfbreed with me had made him understand my question, he rose to his feet and, walking to the edge of a swamp close by, cut three or four reeds, and joining some pieces together, after he had made a hole through the joints, he gently pushed one extremity in a slanting direction into the earth, which he had previously made firm by pressure with his foot; he then cut out a small hole in the clay above the extremity of the reed and, moulding it with his fingers, laughingly said, "Now give me tobacco, and I will show you how to smoke it." He filled the hole with a mixture of tobacco and the bear-berry, placed a live coal on the top and, stretching himself at full length on the ground with his chin supported by both hands, he took the reed between his lips and enjoyed a long smoke.

Henry Youle Hind

Retraining

This change has of necessity forced the Indians into new lines of life, while at the same time it has laid upon our Government increased responsibility in its treatment of the prairie Indians. Food must be furnished for many who, from long habits of dependence upon the buffalo, would starve if no aid were given them. Some of the Indians indeed...take their stand upon the argument: "We had plenty of food until the white man came; now if, as you tell us, the great mother sends her white children here, then, since the buffalo are failing, the great mother must supply us with food." Their creed has at least the merit of simplicity, and, as they have been trained only to hunt and are as yet incapable of maintaining themselves by farming, it is absolutely necessary that the Government should assist in feeding them until they are educated into more settled ways of life. Looked at even as a matter of policy it is cheaper to feed than to fight them, and the latter alternative might be forced upon us if the former were not accepted while, at the same time, this humaner policy would be only in accord with the considerate treatment that has always been shown by the British and Canadian Governments towards the old possessors of the soil.

Rev. Daniel Gordon

Singer

One evening I had a specimen of Indian music from Chantre, the chief Cree singer and drummer of the district. His song, if such it could be called, was a wild dirge-like chant, with no rhythm nor any perceptible air. His performance on the drum, which he kept beating with a small stick, seemed to have no connection whatever with the song except to add to the volume of sound, the drum being a rude form of tambourine. The effect was as confusing as that produced upon the uninitiated in listening to selections from Wagner's *Lohengrin*. In lack of melody, if in no other respect, the Indian music of the past agrees with the German music of the future.

Rev. Daniel Gordon

Red Lake Chippewa Indians at Dufferin, Manitoba, 1872-73. Photo by: Royal Engineers

Graves

Near the fort there is a plain little church used by the R.C. mission and a small graveyard, kept with great neatness. The graves are in almost every case covered by small houses of squared timber, although the bodies have been interred at the usual depth of six feet. In the church we saw a large heavy whip, which is used for punishing those whom the priest condemns, one man being specially set apart to administer the lash.

Rev. Daniel Gordon

Smallpox

Smallpox in its most aggravated type had passed from tribe to tribe, leaving in its track depopulated wigwams and vacant council lodges; thousands (and there are not many thousands, all told) had perished on the great sandy plains that lie between the Saskatchewan and the Missouri. Why this most terrible of diseases should prey with especial fury upon the poor red man of America has never been accounted for by medical authority; but that it does prey upon him with a violence nowhere else to be found is an undoubted fact. Of all the fatal methods of destroying the Indians which his white brother has introduced into the West, this plague of smallpox is the most deadly. The history of its annihilating progress is written in too legible characters on the desolate expanses of untenanted wilds where the Indian graves are the sole traces of the red man's former domination. Beneath this awful scourge whole tribes have disappeared — the bravest and the best have vanished because their bravery forbade that they should flee from the terrible infection and, like soldiers in some square plunged through and rent with shot, the survivors only closed more despairingly together when the death-stroke fell heaviest among them.

William Francis Butler

Magic Charm

One day I saw something hanging on a tree and went to look at it. It consisted of twenty small rods, peeled, and painted red and black, and fastened together on a plane, with cords of bark. A piece of tobacco was placed between the tenth and eleventh rods, and the whole was suspended perpendicularly from a branch of the tree. It belonged to the old chief, who told me that when he was a young man he lay down to dream, and that in his dream the moon spoke to him and told him to make this charm, and to renew it every new moon that he might have a long life. He had regularly done so ever since till the preceding summer when he almost forgot it, and was taken so ill as to be near dying; but he remembered it, his friends did it for him, and he recovered.

Henry Youle Hind

Mourning

Their love, like their hate, goes with them to the grave. They may turn to take a last look upon the tombs of their fathers as they depart; but they will shed no tears, they will heave no groans, for there is in their hearts that which stifles such indications of emotion. It is savage courage absorbed in despair. The lovely valley in which warriors stand forth in their triumphant glory, in which the young and sprightly listen with throbbing hearts to the chants of other days, in which the mothers fondly play with their tender offspring, will soon know them no more. He will recede before the white man as his fathers have done, and at last yield to the inevitable law which decrees that the inferior races shall vanish from the face of the earth, and that the truculent unimprovable savage shall give place to families capable of higher development.

Duncan MacDonald

Chippewa Indian graves and mourners, near Dufferin, Manitoba, c.1873. Photo by: Royal Engineers

Manitoba

It is not hard to trace the sources of all those alarming rumours that we heard so much of at a distance concerning the climate and soil of Manitoba. Our friends on Rat Creek gave us an inkling of them. On their way from St. Paul, Minnesota, with their teams and cattle, at every post they heard those rumours in their most alarming shapes, all of course duly authenticated. They were repeatedly warned not to impoverish their families by going to a cold, locust-devoured, barren land where there was no market and no freedom, but to settle in Minnesota. Agents offered them "the best land in the world" and when, with British stupidity, they shut their ears to all temptations, obstacles were thrown in the way of their going on, and costs and charges so multiplied that the threatened impoverishment would have become a fact before they reached Manitoba had they not been resolute and trusted entirely to their own resources. Even when they arrived at Winnipeg the gauntlet had still to be run. In that "saloon"-crowded village is a knot of touters and indefatigable sympathizers with American institutions, men who had always calculated that our North-west would drop like a ripe pear into the lap of the Republic, who had been at the bottom of the halfbreed insurrection and who are now bitterly disappointed to see their old dream never likely to be more than a dream. These worthies told Grant's party quite confidentially that they had been "so many years" in the country and had not once seen a good crop. Who could doubt such disinterested testimony? It may be asked, what object can these men have in slandering the country and retarding its development? Is not their own interest bound up in its prosperity? Whatever the motives, such are the facts. But the man who would indignantly deny that there is any connection between great schemes on the other side of the boundary line and Winnipeg pot-house politicians has a very poor idea of the thoroughgoing activity of American railway directors and Minnesota land agents.

George Grant

Stagnation

Familiarity with the settlements dispels the favourable impression with which a stranger at first regards them. At a distance the neat whitewashed houses with their gardens and farmyards, continuing without interruption for twenty miles between the forts, the herds of cattle, horses, and sheep feeding on the plains, the vast expanse of what seems to be meadow of the richest description lead one to suppose that universal prosperity and contentment would here be won without anxiety or trouble. Nevertheless, no one can fail to be struck with the indifference to the future which seems habitually to characterize the people, especially the French portion of the population, and to show itself in their unfinished dwellings, neglected farms, and extravagant indulgence in dress or in articles they covet. Many of the apparent efforts of industry which, seen from a distance, excite admiration, shrink upon a nearer approach into sluggish and irregular attempts at improvement, often abandoned before completion. The farms and farm buildings in the occupation of the majority afford no sign of recent improvement; and in general it may be said that the buildings which in Canada would be considered good, roomy, country houses are exclusively possessed and occupied by the retired officers of the Hudson's Bay Company, the traders or merchants of the settlement, and the clergy.

The farmers' homesteads, and the hunters' and trappers' cottages, if these classes here can with propriety be separated, bear rather the appearance of slow decay and a decline in fortune than a healthy, hopeful, progressive condition.

Henry Youle Hind

Offices of the Public Works Department, St. Boniface, Manitoba, 1872-73. Photo by: Royal Engineers

Fort Garry: 1872

But civilization had worked its way even deeper into the Northwest. The place formerly known as Fort Garry had civilized into the shorter denomination of "Garry"; the prairie around the fort had corner lots which sold for more hundreds of dollars than they possessed frontage-feet; and society was divided in opinion as to whether the sale which called forth these prices was a "bogus" one or not.

Representative institutions had been established in the new province of Manitoba, and an election for members of Parliament had just been concluded. Of this triumph of modern liberty over primeval savagery it is sufficient to say that the great principle of freedom of election had been fully vindicated by a large body of upright citizens who, in the freest and most independent manner, had forcibly possessed themselves of the poll booths, and then fired a volley from revolvers or, in the language of the land, "emptied their shooting irons" into another body of equally upright citizens who had the temerity to differ with them as to the choice of a political representative.

It was gently rumoured that some person or persons were to be arrested for this outburst of constitutional patriotism, but any proceeding so calculated to repress the individual independence of the citizen would have been utterly subversive of all representative institutions.

William Francis Butler

Winnipeg: 1880

To give the reader an idea of the progress made by that place since 1870, let us picture to ourselves the impressions of an inhabitant of Winnipeg who at that time had gone to a foreign land, and is returning today to his native country. If he be in Canada or in the United States, he takes a ticket for St. Boniface, situated opposite Winnipeg. Arrived at St. Vincent, he leaves the United States to enter Manitoba. A thousand reminiscences crowd into his mind at the sight of the vast plains on which he had many a time hunted the buffalo. But what impresses and grieves him are the changes which have taken place in those parts. Domesticated cattle have succeeded the buffalo, which have entirely disappeared; the virgin plains, under the effort of settlers, have been partly converted into cultivated fields; wigwams and cabins have given place to elegant houses. Judge of the disappointment of our Manitoban! The farther he advances the more he is pained by the changes that have taken place. Finally the train stops and they call out: "St. Boniface — Winnipeg." He alights from the car and looks around, but the dwellings he beholds resemble in no wise the cabins of former days. The church alone where he attended mass, and which has undergone no change, proves to him that he is at the end of his journey. Mechanically he follows his fellow travellers and, with them, takes the omnibus which crosses Red River on a steam ferry. They pass before the principal hotels of Winnipeg; the omnibus gradually gets rid of passengers. Our Manitoban, finally left alone, asks to be driven to his home; but the omnibus conductor, who however is thoroughly acquainted with the city, declares that he does not know his address. This answer surprises a great deal our traveller. He asks then to be taken to Fort Garry where, in former days, he used to sell his furs to the Hudson's Bay Company. This establishment has so well resisted the hand of progress that our traveller finds at last where he is, and the place where he was born. But his father's home is no more, and on its place is perhaps erected a magnificent building. His discovery only adds to his regrets. His old friends are dead or have emigrated to wild lands; the steamboats have replaced the canoes on Red River; broad streets have succeeded the narrow cart roads; and houses which would do honour to a great city have replaced the Indian wigwams and the log cabins of the halfbreeds. All this is what has been done in ten years! What will be done in ten more?

Jean d'Artigue

Main Street looking south, Winnipeg, Manitoba, 1879. Photo by: Dr. Robert Bell

Red River Transportation Company steamer Selkirk, *c.1873. Photo by: Royal Engineers*

Government House, Upper Fort Garry, Manitoba, c.1876. Photo by: Unknown

Cariole

It grieved me that the men should be exposed to such a storm while I had shelter in the cariole; but I could do nothing to help them, so putting other cares aside I strove to make myself comfortable.

Vain task! Though I buried myself head and all in two robes and a blanket, the wind found its way through everything and I suspect that the master, sitting still in his wraps, suffered more from cold than his men who were running against the bitter hurricane, and suffered besides under the depressing sense of his idle helplessness while they felt the cheering influences of hardy toil.

I hate cariole travelling. It is humiliating to be dragged about in a portable bed like some sick woman while the active voyageurs are maintaining their steady run for hours — for days — for weeks, I daresay, if you required it — for fatigue seems with them an unknown word.

Nevertheless, what must be must, and as from various causes I found myself unable to run for more than a few hours at a time, I was obliged to submit to the luxurious degradation that my very soul abhorred. How different from the days when on my good horse's back I rode rifle in hand, free and confident, equal to any man, and ready for anything!

James Carnegie, Earl of Southesk

Homeward Bound

When nearing a fort you generally strike a firmly pressed snow road, made by hauling in firewood; and the dogs, knowing where they are, always start off at a furious rate which is kept up to the fort, perhaps some eight or ten miles or even more; and should there be any sudden turn in the road round some stump or tree, the sleigh is upset, and then you must walk the rest of the distance as nothing will stop them but the sleigh becoming jammed between two trees, and the chances of this happening are very small.

Charles Messiter

Tried and True

It is said that a high dignitary of the Church was once making a winter tour through his missions in the North-west. The driver, out of deference for his freight's profession, abstained from the use of forcible language to his dogs, and the hauling was very indifferently performed. Soon the train came to the foot of a hill and, notwithstanding all the efforts of the driver with whip and stick, the dogs were unable to draw the cariole to the summit.

"Oh," said the Church dignitary, "this is not at all as good a train of dogs as the one you drove last year; why, they are unable to pull me up this hill!"

"No, monseigneur," replied the owner of the dogs, "but I am driving them differently; if you will only permit me to drive them in the old way you will see how easily they will pull the cariole to the top of this hill; they do not understand my new method."

"By all means," said the bishop, "drive them then in the usual manner."

Instantly there rang out a long stream of "sacré chien," "sacré diable," and still more unmentionable phrases. The effect upon the dogs was magical; the cariole flew to the summit; the progress of the episcopal tour was undeniably expedited, and a practical exposition was given of the poet's thought, "From seeming evil still educing good."

William Francis Butler

Cariole and team, Fort Garry, Manitoba, 1872. Photo by: Charles Horetzky

Norway House from Swan River Rock, Manitoba, 1878. Photo by: Dr. Robert Bell

The operations of the Hudson's Bay Company extend over territories whose inhabitants owe allegiance to three different and independent governments, British, Russian, and the United States. These immense territories exceeding 4,500,000 square miles in area are divided, for the exclusive purposes of the fur trade, into four departments and thirty-three districts, in which are included one hundred and fifty-two posts, commanding the services of three thousand agents, traders, voyageurs, and servants, besides giving occasional or constant employment to about one hundred thousand savage Indian hunters. Armed vessels, both sailing and steam, are employed on the North-west coast to carry on the fur trade with the warlike natives of that distant region. More than twenty years ago the trade of the North-west coast gave employment to about one thousand men, occupying twenty-one permanent establishments, or engaged in navigating five armed sailing vessels and one armed steamer varying from one hundred to three hundred tons in burden. History does not furnish another example of an association of private individuals exerting a powerful influence over so large an extent of the earth's surface, and administering their affairs with such consummate skill and unwavering devotion to the original objects of their incorporation.

Henry Youle Hind

Interior of Norway House, Manitoba, 1878. Photo by: Dr. Robert Bell

The Saulteaux came in with an antelope skin and commenced negotiating with Mr. McKenzie for a sack of vermilion paint in exchange for the skin, though he still wore red war paint and other colours on those parts of his anatomy not covered by his red blanket, breech clout and beaded moccasins. An eagle feather on his head, he had at his waist as further evidence of his bravery a scalping knife with a fresh Sioux scalp dangling beside it.

The transaction completed to his satisfaction, he was about to leave when the French halfbreed entered. Without a sound he seized the Saulteaux's knife and cut him open to the waist so swiftly that our clerk did not see what had happened until the unfortunate customer returned to trade the now useless war paint for some cloth to tie himself together.

When Mr. McKenzie did not understand, the Indian opened his blanket held tightly around him, thereby letting his whole interior fall out on the floor to be instantly covered by his body. In a few seconds his soul was with those of his late victims in the mythical hunting ground that is the destiny of all brave Indians.

His murderer was promptly put in gaol and afterwards tried before Judge Black, convicted of murder and sentenced to be hung by the neck until dead with the usual hope that the Lord would have mercy on his soul.

Walter Traill

Lieut.-Gov. Morris' son with his new Indian pony, Fort Garry, Manitoba, c.1876. Photo by: Unknown

In the morning I borrowed a pony and rode down the river some twelve miles to where the fort band of horses was, an Indian boy going with me to show me the way; and I do not think I ever saw anything more curious than the appearance the prairies where they had been feeding presented. The ponies are turned out late in the autumn and have to shift for themselves until the following April and, if judiciously herded, they will come up quite fat, though this fat is soft and will not last if they are at once worked hard. When the snow becomes deep they scrape a hole and get into it, pawing away the snow till they get at the grass; they will enlarge the hole at the bottom to get as much grass as possible, and when they can reach no more they plunge out and make another hole, the sides of these holes serving as a protection against the cold winds of winter. A prairie after they have left it presents much the appearance of a dilapidated piece of honeycomb.

Charles Messiter

Old Indian camp and grave, Lake of the Woods, Ontario, 1872. Photo by: Royal Engineers

Hayes River at the mouth of Ten Shilling Creek, York Factory, Manitoba, 1880. Photo by: Dr. Robert Bell

Are you ambitious, reader, of dwelling in a "pleasant cot in a tranquil spot, with a distant view of the changing sea"? If so, do not go to York Factory. Not that it is such an unpleasant place — for I spent two years very happily there — but simply (to give a poetical reason, and explain its character in one sentence) because it is a monstrous blot on a swampy spot, with a partial view of the frozen sea!

Robert Ballantyne

PART II
THE PRAIRIES

Provisions

Under charge of this efficient brigade there was gathered together a very considerable amount of property of every sort and kind — horses and vehicles, weapons, provisions, and stores: three new two-wheel carts and the four-wheel wagon already mentioned, all filled to the brim with various sorts of baggage; my own canvas tent (the same one I had used before), a large bell tent for the men, oilcloth squares, blankets, clothes and other personal goods; bales of tea and sugar, sacks of flour and rice; biscuits, jam, and eggs, and dried tongues in plenty to keep us in food till we got fresh meat in the buffalo country; many pounds of the Company's excellent flat "plug" tobacco for myself and my men; an immense 90 lb. roll of the rather coarser twist for the especial benefit of the Indians.

Then we had a great quantity of goods of another description such as a large copper box of rifle powder, kegs of common powder, bullets, shot, and caps; a variety of weapons; axes, hammers, saws, a canteen, a portable table and a camp-stool, cooking utensils, etc.; in short, we were provided with more than every requisite for the plains, besides extra supplies to furnish the customary presents to any Indian parties we might chance to meet.

James Carnegie, Earl of Southesk

Prairie Storm

At four p.m. we started for the next post, Rat Creek, ten miles off. The sky was threatening but, as we always disregarded appearances, no one proposed a halt. On the open prairie, when just well away from the Hudson's Bay Company's store, we saw that we were in for a storm. Every form of beauty was combined in the sky at this time. To the south it was such blue as Titian loved to paint: blue, that those who have seen only dull English skies say is nowhere to be seen but on canvas or in heaven; and the blue was bordered to the west with vast billowy mountains of the softest, fleeciest white. Next to that, and right ahead of us, and overhead, was a swollen black cloud along the undersurface of which greyer masses were eddying at a terrific rate. Extending from this, and all around the north and east, the expanse was a dun-coloured mass livid with lightning and there, to the right, and behind us, torrents of rain were pouring and nearing us every moment. The atmosphere was charged with electricity on all sides, lightning rushed towards the earth in straight and zigzag currents, and the thunder varied from the sharp rattle of musketry to the roar of artillery; still there was no rain and but little wind. We pressed on for a house, not far away; but there was to be no escape. With the suddenness of a tornado the wind struck us — at first without rain — but so fierce that the horses were forced again and again off the track. And now with the wind came rain, thick and furious; and then hail — hail mixed with angular lumps of ice from half an inch to an inch across, a blow on the head from one of which was stunning. Our long line of horses and carts was broken. Some of the poor creatures clung to the road, fighting desperately; others were driven into the prairie and, turning their backs to the storm, stood still or moved sideways with cowering heads, their manes and long tails floating wildly like those of Highland shelties. . . . In half an hour we got under the shelter of the log house a mile distant; but the fury of the storm was past, and in less than an hour the sun burst forth again, scattering the clouds, till not a blot was left in the sky save fragments of mist to the south and east.

George Grant

Ox train at Dead Horse Creek, west of Pembina, Manitoba, 1873-74. Photo by: Royal Engineers

Prairie Fire

The latter part of the autumn season had not passed without one or two incidents worthy of record. The heat of the sun and the excessive drought during the summer had completely parched the prairie grass, and the soil was fissured in all directions. Although the greatest vigilance was practised, the occurrence of prairie fires seemed inevitable, and towards the end of August a pillar of smoke visible to the north, a great distance off, gave warning that before many days were past the whole of the Great Plains would be swept by fire. The course of the fire was most capricious and often turned by a ravine, or by a slight change in the wind, into a new course. The onward progress of the fire was noticed for many days by the gradually-increasing temperature of the air, and soon by the smell of the burning grass. The various parties of the Boundary Comission, being scattered over 400 miles of longitude at the same time, experienced very varied fortune in their encounter with the fire. A surveying party working in one of the ravines five or six miles from their camp found that the fire had swept round behind them and threatened their camp with destruction. They had just time to reach their camp and to tear down their tents, and to plunge everything into an adjoining pool to save their camp equipage, and much was partially destroyed. A commissariat wagon train drawn by oxen was also overtaken by the fire, and though a burnt patch of ground was prepared and the oxen released from the wagons and driven to it, the unfortunate animals were too much alarmed to remain quiet, but rushed about wildly in the flames and were badly singed about the legs. One of the men had the hair on his face burnt and, in the rush of wind accompanying the passage of the fire, his hat went away, adding fuel to the flames. At one of the astronomical camps one of the officers, seeing the onward progress of the fire, employed all the men in the camp to meet the fire and save as much grass as possible by burning a strip; this was so far successful that about 400 acres of grass were saved, which were of incalculable value to the transport animals on the final retreat; but the fire that had been started with this object at last got beyond control, and swept back upon their own camp and nearly destroyed it. On one occasion one of the labourers thoughtlessly struck a match on his boot in a patch of long grass and in an instant the fire flew, and though the camp was saved, the effect of that fire was afterwards ascertained to have destroyed the grass for 150 miles of longitude and then to have turned southwards, when it is probable its progress in that direction was not arrested till it reached the Missouri River. The result of all these prairie fires, which raged in different localities between the middle of August and middle of September, was that the general appearance of the country was now changed from the universal yellow tint to a dismal black, and the whole surface of the plains was as bare of herbage as the sand on the seashore. The homeward march was consequently rendered doubly anxious by the want of fodder for the horses and oxen; but by diligent search patches of grass in marshy places were found where the fire could not reach, and to such places mowers would be sent with light wagons to cut as much grass as they could find during the day's march and bring it to the main body later on in the day at the camping ground.

Samuel Anderson

Sappers building boundary mound, 1873. Photo by: Royal Engineers

49

On Pemmican

As the word pemmican is one which may figure frequently in these pages, a few words explanatory of it may be useful. Pemmican, the favourite food of the Indian and the halfbreed voyageur, can be made from the flesh of any animal but it is nearly altogether composed of buffalo meat; the meat is first cut into slices, then dried either by fire or in the sun and then pounded or beaten out into a thick flaky substance; in this state it is put into a large bag made from the hide of the animal, the dry pulp being soldered down into a hard solid mass by melted fat being poured over it — the quantity of fat is nearly half the total weight, forty pounds of fat going to fifty pounds of "beat meat"; the best pemmican generally has added to it ten pounds of berries and sugar, the whole composition forming the most solid description of food that man can make. If any person should feel inclined to ask, "What does pemmican taste like?" I can only reply, "Like pemmican"; there is nothing else in the world that bears to it the slightest resemblance. Can I say anything that will give the reader an idea of its sufficing quality? Yes, I think I can. A dog that will eat from four to six pounds of raw fish a day when sleighing will only devour two pounds of pemmican, if he be fed upon that food; yet I have seen Indians and halfbreeds eat four pounds of it in a single day — but this is anticipating. Pemmican can be prepared in many ways, and it is not easy to decide which method is the least objectionable. There is rubeiboo and richot, and pemmican plain and pemmican raw, this last method being the one most in vogue amongst voyageurs, but the richot, to me, seemed the best; mixed with a little flour and fried in a pan, pemmican in this form can be eaten, provided the appetite be sharp and there is nothing else to be had — this last consideration is, however, of importance.

William Francis Butler

Had "berry-pemmican" at supper. That is to say, the ordinary buffalo pemmican with Saskootoom berries sprinkled through it at the time of making — which acts as currant jelly does with venison, correcting the greasiness of the fat by a slightly acid sweetness..... Berry-pemmican is usually the best of its kind, but poor at the best. Take scrapings from the driest outside corner of a very stale piece of cold roast beef, add to it lumps of tallowy rancid fat, then garnish all with long human hairs (on which string pieces, like beads upon a necklace) and short hairs of oxen, or dogs, or both — and you have a fair imitation of common pemmican, though I should rather suppose it to be less nasty.

James Carnegie, Earl of Southesk

Log Cabin

We got on very slowly with our house and were wondering how we were going to raise the higher logs when an immense halfbreed called Tom Boot happened to come along, and we engaged him to help us. This man being six feet seven inches high, and the biggest man in every way I ever saw, could lift a log by himself which Badger and I staggered under, and our house was soon built.

We made a door of a portion of our cart and put in a parchment window made of deer hide, inserting one small pane of glass, the only one they could spare me at the fort, in the middle of it; then we made some very rough stools and a table out of more of the cart, and put down a floor of pine logs, each log making one board, as we had no saw — a plan I cannot recommend as being on economical principles.

Then came the chimney. Oh! that chimney! I think it took as long to build as the whole house. We would get it up about halfway, and in the morning find that it had fallen down again in the night. There were no stones about and no proper clay, so we had to work grass into the mud to make it stand. We made it across a corner, as being easier to build there, and left a large space for a fire, five feet square, in which we had some splendid ones during the winter. Why it did not take fire I cannot imagine, as we had put in any number of sticks to keep it up and there was as much grass as mud in its composition.

Charles Messiter

Bad Day

Monday, September 22nd — A most unlucky day. I commence by burning my boots and socks which were drying by the lodge fire. After starting with Messiter to walk ahead I find I have lost the top of the shot bag Milton lent me. I then miss five ducks in succession and fire three barrels at snipe without success. I give up shooting and rejoin the carts. See a badger running along the road in front of me. Milton and I give chase. I get within thirty yards and give him a charge of No. 3; it turns him over and he stops and grins at me; other barrel not loaded from losing shot bag. I run after him and turn him repeatedly, trying to cram in a charge of buckshot in gun. Voudrie comes up and hits him over nose with switch but he succeeds in getting to earth to my chagrin, as I hoped to begin my hunt. Rain coming on, camp about 5:30 having made a short day.

Walter Cheadle

Turtle Mountain Depot, Manitoba, 1873. Photo by: Royal Engineers

Dead Men

Leading from the buffalo pound in two diverging rows, the bushes they designate "dead men" and which serve to guide the buffalo when at full speed were arranged. The "dead men" extended a distance of four miles into the prairie west of and beyond the Sand Hills. They were placed about fifty feet apart, and between the extremity of the rows might be a distance of from one and a half to two miles.

When the skilled hunters are about to bring in a herd of buffalo from the prairie, they direct the course of the gallop of the alarmed animals by confederates stationed in hollows or small depressions who, when the buffalo appear inclined to take a direction leading from the space marked out by the "dead men," show themselves for a moment and wave their robes, immediately hiding again. This serves to turn the buffalo slightly in another direction and when the animals, having arrived between the rows of "dead men," endeavour to pass through them, Indians here and there stationed behind a "dead man" go through the same operation and thus keep the animals within the narrowing limits of the converging lines.

Paul Kane

Buffalo Pound

December 26 — This morning we were off by 4:30 a.m., and had gone a considerable distance when we saw fresh traces of Indians, and soon heard the bawling and screaming of an immense camp, all in a high state of excitement. Diverging from our path to pay them a visit, we found that they had succeeded in driving a large band of buffalo into their "pound" during the night and were now engaged in slaughtering them. The scene was more repulsive than pleasant or exciting. The pound is a circular strong fencing about fifty yards in diameter made of stakes with boughs interlaced, and into this place were crammed more than 100 buffalo bulls, cows, and calves. A great number were already killed and the live ones were tumbling about furiously over the dead bodies of their companions, and I hardly think the space would have held them all alive without some being on top of the others and, in addition, the bottom of the pound was strewn with fragments of carcasses left from former slaughters in the same place. It was on a slope, and the upper part of the fencing was increased in height by skins stretched on poles for the purpose of frightening the buffalo from jumping out. This is not needed at the lower part of the enclosure, as the animals always endeavour to jump uphill. The entrance to the enclosure is by an inclined plane made of rough logs leading to a gap through which the buffalo have suddenly to jump about six feet into the ring so that they cannot return. To this entrance converge lines of little heaps of buffalo dung or brush from several miles into the prairies which surround the clump of wood in which the pound is concealed. These lines serve to lead the buffalo in the required direction when they have been driven into the neighbourhood. When first captured and driven into the pound, which difficult matter is effected by stratagem, the buffalo run round and round violently and, the Indians affirm, always with the sun. Crouched on the fencing were the Indians, even mere boys and young girls, all busy plying bows and arrows, guns and spears and even knives to compass the destruction of the buffalo. After firing their arrows they generally succeeded in extracting them again by a noose on the end of a pole, and some had even the pluck to jump into the area and pull them out with their hands; but if an old bull or a cow happened to observe them they had to be very active in getting out again. The scene was a busy but a bloody one, and has to be carried on until every animal is killed to enable them to get the meat. I helped by trying the penetrating power of rifle balls on the shaggy skulls of the animals, with invariable success; and it is the least cruel way of killing them, as they drop at once. There are many superstitions connected with the whole business, and the Indians always consider their success in procuring buffalo in this manner to depend on the pleasure of the Manitou, to whom they always make offerings which they place under the entrance to the pound where I saw a collection of Indian valuables, among which were bridles, powder horns, tobacco, beads, and the like placed there by the believing Indians, only to be stolen by the first scamp in the camp who could manage the theft adroitly. In the centre of the pound also there is a tall pole on which they hang offerings. To which piece of idolatry I was in a manner accessory by giving them my pocket handkerchief to convert into a flag.

John Palliser

Wigwam, an Ojibway halfbreed, Red River Settlements, Manitoba, 1858. Photo by: Humphrey Lloyd Hime

Solitude

Around [these hills], far into endless space, stretch immense plains of bare and scanty vegetation, plains seared with the tracks of countless buffalo which, until a few years ago, were wont to roam in vast herds between the Assiniboine and the Saskatchewan. Upon whatever side the eye turns when crossing these great expanses, the same wrecks of the monarch of the prairie lie thickly strewn over the surface. Hundreds of thousands of skeletons dot the short scant grass; and when fire has laid barer still the level surface, the bleached ribs and skulls of long-killed bison whiten far and near the dark burnt prairie. There is something unspeakably melancholy in the aspect of this portion of the North-west. From one of the westward jutting spurs of these hills the eye sees far away over an immense plain; the sun goes down, and as he sinks upon the earth the straight line of the horizon becomes visible for a moment across his blood-red disc, but so distant, so far away, that it seems dream-like in its immensity. There is not a sound in the air or on the earth; on every side lie spread the relics of the great fight waged by man against the brute creation; all is silent and deserted — the Indian and the buffalo gone, the settler not yet come. You turn quickly to the right or left; over a hilltop, close by, a solitary wolf steals away. Quickly the vast prairie begins to grow dim and darkness forsakes the skies because they light their stars, coming down to seek in the utter solitude of the blackened plains a kindred spirit for the night.

William Francis Butler

Plague

Suddenly I was aware of a heavy black cloud on the western horizon which looked like an approaching storm but the sky around me remained clear and, thinking it was a prairie fire in the distance, I rode on until dusk. On the way home I again passed the barley field and it was not too dark to see that it was now a blackened ruin.

"Did you have a fire?" I asked the watchman who opened the gates for me. "The barley for our saddle horses is all burned."

"We had no fire," he said. "Did you not see the grasshoppers?"

Then I looked around and saw them three inches deep inside the fort. They had devoured everything in the garden except roots, stripped the trees, and had fallen in the lake until the outlet was blocked, and they were piled up on its shores in windrows.

To prevent them from filling the fort I had to keep half the men in double shifts carting them out in order to live. The ducks and prairie chicken ate grasshoppers until they were unfit for us to eat. Even the eggs tasted of them. The train dogs got fat and the cattle became poor for lack of grass. The whole valley looked like a burned-over prairie. They came in clouds like smoke and for twelve days the air was alive with them as high as one could see. They darkened the sun and lay an inch thick on the ground. The lakes and rivers stink with the dead ones. The frost has at last killed them and some of the vegetables they left. Farming here is all a delusion.

Walter Traill

Captain Featherstonehaugh's camp at Pyramid, Saskatchewan, 1873-74. Photo by: Royal Engineers

Indian Camp

About twenty more Indians came in to have a look at me and all of them shook hands, which was a good sign. I was given a big plateful of boiled buffalo meat and some tea, and soon felt much better. I then made signs that I wished to change my clothes, which were soaking wet, and put on a blanket, and that the women had better go out while I did so, on which they all laughed, and the women crowded round and helped me to undress, pinching and slapping me when they had done so. They gave me a buffalo robe and blanket, which latter I put on Indian fashion, and felt almost one of themselves.

I soon turned in, hoping to have a good night, or rather morning, for it was now nearly five a.m. But alas! for the plans of mice and men! I had not quite gone off to sleep when I began to feel something biting me, and this feeling spread till I fancied I must be on fire, so I jumped up and found that it was only the usual inhabitants of an Indian's buffalo robe feasting on something softer than they usually got. On my telling the Indians what the matter was they laughed, and said I should soon get used to it; but not believing this I got up and put on some of my half-dried garments, and lay down again thinking that now my troubles were over, instead of which they were only beginning.

There are some few peculiarities about an Indian camp which very much interfere with the repose of anyone who is not used to them. The first thing which woke me once more was the pressure of the feet of some animals passing over me; then came a number of others of the same kind, and these seemed to go round and round the tent. It struck me almost immediately that they were dogs hunting for scraps, so I pulled my robe closer round me and dozed off again. Presently, however, I heard a yell followed by a rush and the dogs passed over me again, followed by a furious squaw whose big flat feet were not at all particular where they trod; and this happened several times till I felt as if I was lying in the sawdust of a circus, with the whole performance going on on top of me. I moved at once, getting as close to the side of the lodge as I could, or I should have been flattened out, squaws as a rule being very clumsy and heavy. What made the chase last so long was the difficulty of finding the door, which was small, and as it was dark outside did not show at all.

On the departure of the dogs I thought I should have peace, but I was mistaken; the noise had woke up an Indian, who fancied that he could, with an effort, eat a little more, so he proceeded to get up and cook some meat on the fire in the centre of the lodge and, thinking he had a fine voice which should be cultivated, he sang all the time. This roused a second Indian to do the same thing, and it was almost morning when I really got off to sleep.

Sometimes there are other pleasant surprises for the visitor to a lodge such as a disconsolate widow going round the camp bewailing her lost husband, which she is supposed to do for six months unless she gets another in the meantime. He may have beaten her every day with a lodge-pole and she may have been delighted to have got rid of him, but she must nevertheless go through this performance, and it is always done at night. Then, too, some Indian often gets up and sings for an hour or more, beating an accompaniment on a tom-tom, and no one thinks of sending for a policeman or shooting him, as would seem natural.

Charles Messiter

Sioux Indians at Turtle Mountain, Manitoba, 1873-74. Photo by: Royal Engineers

Fort Carlton, Saskatchewan, 1871. Photo by: Charles Horetzky

58

Interior of Fort Carlton, Saskatchewan, 1871. Photo by: Charles Horetzky

I hate the sight of these forts. Strange, large tumbledown places, like lumber rooms on a vast scale. All the white men living in them look as if they had been buried for a century or two and dug up again and had scarcely yet got their eyes open, for they look frightened when they see a stranger! The women are masses of fat and speak nothing but Cree; and dogs and Indians wander about the large, dark, and filthy courtyards at pleasure — the latter so noiselessly with their moccasined feet that, when you sometimes sit down to write alone, on looking up you find a circle of wild faces fixed upon you, watching everything you do with great attention. Then no one can conceive the nuisance of the dogs. Each fort has a hundred or two of these devils which, Harriott tells me, are necessary for the winter sleighing, and these roam about searching for food (they are never fed), the courtyard being a perpetual scene of growling, snarling, and yelping all day, and of lamentable howling choruses all night. The plains, the plains for me!

Frederick Graham

Benevolence

I am not one of those who find fault with everything that the Hudson's Bay Company does, nor do I believe that business cannot be carried on under their "monopoly", as some term it. They have been the pioneers of civilization in these back settlements, and they have shown the greatest kindness and humanity towards the Indian tribes when the Americans shot them down like dogs for mere amusement, considering it a very good joke to shoot one at long range and see him jump as the fatal bullet pierced his heart. It is utterly absurd to say that the Hudson's Bay Company is an obstacle to the development of the country.

Duncan MacDonald

Firewater

It is a mistake to suppose that spirits are supplied to the Indians in large quantity from the Company's stores. In the northern districts spirits are not allowed to enter the country; and in no case are they a medium of traffic for furs, though in the southern districts rum is exchanged for provisions, which cannot be got on other terms.

James Carnegie, Earl of Southesk

The old fellow rejoiced in the name of Kekek-ooarsis, or "the child of the hawk," in allusion to the beak-like form of his nose. We smoked several pipes with him .... and were so delighted with his urbanity that in a weak moment we promised to make him a present of a small quantity of rum. Alas! mistaken generosity, fruitful of anxiety and trouble! The old gentleman became all excitement, said we were the best fellows he had met for many a day, adding that if he might venture to offer a suggestion, it would be that we should fetch the firewater immediately. We accordingly went back to the lodge, sent off to him a very small quantity well watered, taking the precaution to fill a small keg with a weak mixture and hiding the cask in the cart.

It does not answer, however, to dilute the spirits too much. It must be strong enough to be inflammable, for an Indian always tests it by pouring a few drops into the fire. If it possesses the one property from which he has given it the name of firewater, he is satisfied, whatever its flavour or other qualities may be.

We had hardly covered up the cask when Kekek-ooarsis appeared, accompanied by his squaw, a withered old hag, and Keenamontiayoo, "the long neck," his son-in-law. The men were already half drunk, singing away the Indian song without words, and clamorous for more rum. They produced a number of marten and other skins, and all our explanations failed to make them understand that we had not come as traders.

After two hours' continued discussion, we doled out another small quantity as the only way to get rid of them. How they chuckled and hugged the pot exclaiming, "Tarpwoy! tarpwoy!" (It is true! it is true!), hardly able to believe the delightful fact. At the first dawn of day they entered the lodge again, bringing more furs for sale.

Boys rode off as couriers in all directions to carry the welcome tidings to their friends in the neighbourhood. Before long, men came galloping up from different quarters, and these were presently followed by squaws and children, all eager to taste the pleasure-giving firewater, and our lodge was soon crowded with importunate guests .... First one fellow thrust a marten skin into our hands, another two or three fish, while a third, attempting to strip off his shirt for sale, fell senseless into the arms of his squaw. The demand was the same with all, and incessant: "Isquitayoo arpway! isquitayoo arpway!" (Firewater! firewater!) Hour after hour we sat smoking our pipes with an air of unconcern we did not feel, and refusing all requests. Afternoon came and the scene still continued. We dared not leave the lodge lest they should search the carts and discover our store.

Wearily passed the time till darkness came on and still the crowd sat round, and still the same request was dinned into our ears. But we were thoroughly determined not to give way, and at last they began to conclude we were inexorable, and dropped off one by one, immensely disgusted with our meanness.

Milton and Cheadle

Group at Medicine Hat, Alberta, 1885. Photo by: O.B. Buell

Credit

It was a stormy day when a Saulteaux, Keech-ben-nees, came into our store to negotiate the sale of a bearskin for a blanket in trade. "A very big, black bear," he assured me it was, "worth twenty-four shillings." I went into our storehouse and selected a blanket valued at twenty shillings and for the other four shillings he chose a warm red shirt, but made no move to produce the bearskin. In regard to the delicate matter of payment he said he would bring it to me in four days.

"But Big Bird," I asked in surprise, "why do you not bring it with you now?"

In mixed Saulteaux and English he finally conveyed to me the startling information that his cash in hand was still at large, as he had not yet killed the bear. His stoical countenance portrayed not the slightest concern when he could not say exactly where the bear might be, but solemnly declared he had seen its tracks in the snow bordering Red Deer Creek.

Walter Traill

White Cloud

We found at the "Post" — as all forts are usually called — a Scotchman named Alexander who, having tried a great many things and failed at all of them, had ended by becoming a Hudson's Bay Company's clerk at twenty-four pounds a year and his food. Having some relics of his departed greatness yet with him, he went about in an old velvet dressing-jacket bound with gold cord, with a cap of the same material on his head, and being a fine man and very handsome, he looked quite imposing and was the admiration of all the squaws.

One day I heard a story of him which is worth inserting here. It seems that the Sioux and Cree Indians wished to make peace, and it had been arranged that they should do so at the Post. Accordingly the Sioux chief White Cloud arrived with seventeen warriors and camped outside the stockade, the Crees having also sent a deputation to meet him, and while the preparations were being completed, White Cloud — who was a splendidly made Indian, standing over six feet in his moccasins, with a really fine face — almost lived in the fort. He was one day in Alexander's room when the latter took up some boxing gloves and put them on, telling White Cloud that these were the things with which the white man learned to fight, asking the chief if he would like to put them on. White Cloud of course had no idea of what would happen, for Indians never hit with the hands, and to hit one of them is to insult him most grossly. White Cloud said he should like to try them, so Alexander first took away his knife and pistol and locked them up; then putting him in the middle of the room and telling him to stand on his guard, he knocked him to the other end of it and, on his rising and rushing at Alexander, he was again sent to the same place. His rage I was told more resembled madness and, tearing off the gloves, he tried to get his knife from the drawer; but finding it locked he suddenly calmed down, or seemed to do so, and demanded to be let out. Alexander asked him what he would do when outside, when White Cloud told him that he and his men would instantly attack the fort and kill everyone in it.

Seeing that only desperate measures would have a chance of succeeding here, Alexander took a revolver from a drawer and told the chief that unless he promised within five minutes to give up his intention and make friends, he would shoot him and chance what came of it. For some minutes White Cloud was obstinate, and then seeing that Alexander meant what he said, and being somewhat tempted by some presents which were promised him, he shook hands and, receiving his pistol and knife, left the room, carrying with him two bottles of whisky, for which an Indian will do anything, and which they have no means of getting in the Hudson's Bay territories as they forbid its sale to the Indians. Though never friendly again with Alexander, the chief kept his word, and no harm resulted from this foolish joke.

Charles Messiter

Big Bear trading at Fort Pitt, Saskatchewan, 1885. Photo by: O.B. Buell

Red River Carts

It is a novel sight and rather a picturesque one too to witness a procession of carts, each one drawn by a single ox harnessed into shafts after the manner of a dray-horse. A single man called a "bull driver" takes charge of eight or ten carts and manages his team, aided by a whip (and, by the way, a person requires a vast amount of practice to be able to use "a bull flogger" cleverly). A young larch tree is usually selected for the haft, which should be six feet long and as pliant as a salmon rod; the thong is made of plaited green hide, and should be two inches in diameter at the centre or "belly" of the thong, tapering towards each end, and about three feet to three feet six inches in length. The crack of this whip in the hands of an experienced "bull driver" is like the report of a rifle. Woe betide the unfortunate bullock that gets a real taste of the thong; it takes off the hair like a hot iron and raises a wale as large as a sausage. The oxen are harnessed betwixt shafts like horses, and each ox and its cart will transport a load of eight hundred or a thousand pounds weight. The cart is constructed mostly of wood, and very little if any iron is used in its building. Regular trains of these primitive ox-carts follow the buffalo hunters for the purpose of carting home the hides and meat for preserving. The creaking of the wheels, the cracking of the whips, and the continual shouting of the bull drivers, cheering and abusing their teams by turns, may be heard when they are miles away.

John Keast Lord

Dream

As we were now approaching the neighbourhood of these Indians, Inspector Jarvis recommended the sentries to be carefully on their watch, and the others to sleep with their arms loaded. After leaving Roche Percée, I did not sleep in the tents with the other men, preferring to sleep outside, under a wagon or a tree. And that night, after spreading my blankets under a wagon, I laid down, placing my loaded carbine on my right side, and my revolver on my left. Pondering for a while on the narrative I had heard from the guide, I, at last, went to sleep, and began to dream. I dreamed that we were encamped where we were in reality; that I was under a wagon, and I saw Indians crawling like snakes through the grass and coming towards the camp. Taking hold of my carbine, I tried to rise, but in vain, I could not move. I then attempted

to shout, but could give no utterance. I was in great agony, which was increasing as the Indians were getting nearer and nearer. Already I could see their painted faces, their naked breasts, and their heads adorned with hair and quills. When within fifty yards of the camp they suddenly made a bound which was followed by fearful yells that no pen can describe. Death stared me in the face. I collected all my strength to rise, and this time succeeded so well, that I fell back senseless to the ground, having knocked my head against the axle of the wagon. When my senses returned, I was still lying on my back, the carbine grasped in my right hand, and the revolver in my left. Everything was still with the exception of the horses which were tied to the wagons and eating the grass we had mowed for them the night before. This was only a dream, but of such a horrible nature I did not care for a recurrence of it.

Jean d'Artigue

Indian Territory

July 20th — Continued our journey; found the ground very much broken, and the travelling very severe for the horses. Soil worthless. Found a human skull on the plain. Two Blood Indian chiefs, very fine young men with noble carriage and intelligent countenances, rode up followed by other Indians; they promised to give me a horse each if I would dress them. I gave them coats, and desired Amoxapeta's wife to make the cloth into leggings, and in short we dressed them completely. They thought themselves very fine, but to anyone observing their awkward constrained appearance now, contrasted with the easy dignity with which they made up to greet us clothed in their own apparel a short while previous, would indeed have considered the change one for the worse. We camped on a swamp, where we killed several rattlesnakes.

July 24th — The Indians told us there was now a great deal of sickness among them, and they requested me to come into camp and pray for them that the sickness might be removed. I complied, and read the general confession and the Lord's prayer, which Felix translated into Blackfoot after me. A woman brought a child to the Doctor, which was in a fit, and while he was occupied in making up some medicine for it the medicine man, who had interfered yesterday, came in in a similar manner and attempted to take away the child. The mother of the child, however, aware of the result of the medicine man's exertions in the case of the child which occurred yesterday, flew like a tigress on the medicine man and effectually prevented all interference with Hector. The child recovered.

John Palliser

Railway survey camp at the Elbow of the North Saskatchewan River, Saskatchewan, 1871. Photo by: Charles Horetzky

65

Turning Back

July 7th — Prepared to start the expedition once more; very great unwillingness on the part of the French halfbreeds to move. Old Paul came to me and declared off, saying he was exceedingly sorry to leave me, pleading the commands of his "mother-in-law" as an excuse but, in fact, terrified at the prospects of travelling through the heart of the Blackfoot country. I remonstrated in vain, and at last had nothing for it but to give him leave to go; no sooner was that the case than all the other French halfbreeds commenced to signify their intentions of turning back also. I replied that I granted leave to Paul on account of his family, and on account of his long previous services to the expedition; also to his nephew Moise to accompany him, because he could not well get on without him; but that I would not allow anyone else to leave the camp: a slight murmur of disapprobation then arose concerning this decision, and before they had time to get together or combine, I exclaimed, "Who is the first man who will say that he will turn back?" upon which, one bolder than the rest stood up and exclaimed, "I will go back." I rushed right at him, and seized him by the throat, and shook him, and then, catching him by the collar, kicked him out of the camp. I called out then to know if any other wished also to go back but, fortunately, the retrograde movement extended no further. Started at once for Bull Pond Creek.

John Palliser

Torture

Two days' more travelling brought us to the South Saskatchewan, both this and the main river being solidly frozen over so that we had no difficulty in crossing, and here we found a large camp of Crees who were much excited about the capture of a Sioux Indian by some members of the tribe; the Sioux and Crees being once more at war, as the peace which had been made at Fort Carlton had lasted only one summer.

On our arrival we were given a small lodge by an Indian who turned one of his wives out of it, and when we had put our saddles, packs, etc. in it and placed a boy to watch them, we went to pay a visit to Big Bear, the head chief. We found him in his lodge holding a council as to what should be done with the Sioux, and he hardly noticed us till this was over, when he informed me through Badger, on my inquiring as to the man's fate, that he was to be tortured on the next day but one. I remonstrated and offered to buy him from them, giving everything I had with me, but to no purpose, and I left vowing vengeance which I had no means of executing.

On the following morning I got leave to see the prisoner whom I found to be almost a boy, very small and weak-looking but perfectly calm, though he had been told what his fate was to be. Badger managed to make him understand that I was trying to save him, on which he shook hands with me, but seemed to think he must die.

I went to see the chief again in the afternoon and had a long talk with him, adding to my previous offers if he would let me have the Sioux, but he assured me he had really no power in the matter. During the night I went near the lodge several times in which the Sioux was confined, hoping to get him out in the dark, but always found it guarded and was ordered back.

In the morning we left the camp as we did not wish to see the torturing done, and late at night we reached a small band of Chippewas who were out on a hunt and remained with them three days — seeing a good many buffalo, but finding the running very bad as there had been a light fall of snow so all holes were covered, and I got one very bad fall in consequence. We loaded all the ponies with meat and started on our return journey leading them, and on the morning of the third day we reached the Cree camp once more and found it deserted; but in the middle of it stood a big stake to which was bound all that remained of the Sioux prisoner, and a horrible sight it was. They had cut off his hands and feet with Indian hatchets, taking perhaps ten or twelve blows for each limb; then he was scalped, his tongue was cut out, and one of his feet was forced into his mouth, which had been slit to admit it, and he was stuck full of small spikes of wood, most of these horrible tortures, I was afterwards told, being done by the women. We buried him as well as we could with our hunting knives and, proceeding on our journey, reached home safely.

Charles Messiter

Crow Indians killed by Piegan Indians, Sweetgrass Hills, Montana, 1873. Photo by: Royal Engineers

Cree camp south of Vermilion, Alberta, 1871. Photo by: Charles Horetzky

Cooking at Turtle Mountain Depot, Manitoba, c.1873. Photo by: Royal Engineers

Buckskin

Sioux Chief Long Dog and George Wells (NWMP), Fort Walsh, Saskatchewan, 1879. Photo by: George Anderton

This style of dress is decidedly showy and picturesque, and having said so much of it, I have exhausted everything that it is possible to say in its praise. I know of no good quality belonging to a leather hunting suit; but such as are objectionable I could multiply *ad infinitum*. It is disagreeably heavy without supplying an equivalent of warmth. Assuming the character of tripe or a damp chamois leather when saturated with wet it becomes, when in that state, cold, clammy, and uncomfortable beyond description.

Then when you have succeeded in drying the suit, a work of time even if aided by the sun or the campfire or both, you have to robe yourself in garments much like a light armour of lantern-horn; your "pants" in all probability will have receded into the breeches pattern, and the sleeves of your jacket have modestly retired to the region of the elbow. I care not how much tugging and stretching you may bestow on your wet suit of leather, shrink it will though you do your "darndest" to prevent it; not only that, but it shrinks (without being wetted externally) day after day from perspiration. One observes his "pants" are creeping steadily away from off the insteps; as the tide during its ebb leaves rock after rock exposed, so the leather steals away from the hands and feet, gradually uncovering at first wrists and ankles, then arms and legs; and if some curative means were not resorted to, I verily believe the pants would become like to those worn by acrobats and tight-rope dancers, and the jacket sleeves dwindle into mere armlets such as ladies wear when in evening dress. If nothing better can be obtained, there is no other course left open than that of wearing leather or going *à la sauvage*, "sans" everything. But adopt my advice, and never wear leather if you can help it.

John Keast Lord

North West Mounted Police Officers at Fort Walsh, Saskatchewan, c.1876. Photo by: Unknown

November 13th — Corporal Heney returned from Benton with a cargo of whisky and there was a great drunk in the barracks.

14th — Const. Workman of C and Const. Hanfine of E Troop got fined $10 for breaking barracks and one month confined to barracks.

15th — Const. Conroy of E Troop was fined $10 and one month to barracks for being drunk. Wall James was fined $10 for being drunk downtown. Capt. Frechette and Capt. McIllree and Dr. Kennedy were drunk today. Sgt. Major Bray has took on for three years more.

16th — A fight took place downtown at Mick Walter's be-

tween the Police and citizens. We got orders to clean the house out and we put them out pretty quick. It commenced by a citizen calling Const. J. Daley a bad name and we went for them. Most of the boys were drunk, this happened about nine o'clock at night. Capt. Winder came down and stopped it but he said as much as to go for them.

18th — Capt. Winder and Capt. McIllree and Capt. Frechette were drunk all day and night. Const. Larkins was drunk and had five gallons of wine, also Corporal Ryan and Const. Paterson, also the citizens.

Const. Simon Clarke, NWMP

Métis

Fervently as I wished them away, it cheered one's spirits to see the hunters on their march. There was infinite picturesqueness about them. Their long moving columns sparkled with life and gaiety. Cart-tilts of every hue flashed brightly in the sun, hosts of wild wolfish dogs ran in and out among the vehicles, troops of loose horses pranced and galloped alongside. The smartly-dressed men were riding their showiest steeds, their wives and daughters were travelling in the carts, enthroned on high heaps of baggage. Many of the women were clearly of unmingled Indian blood. Tall and angular, long masses of straight black hair fell over their backs; blue and white cotton gowns, shapeless, stayless, uncrinolined, displayed the flatness of their unprojecting figures. Some wore a gaudy handkerchief on the head, the married bound one also across the bosom.

In M. B —— 's first cart there sat a singularly handsome girl, a dark-complexioned maiden of the mixed French descent. As with so many of her race, her countenance bore a half-shy, half-disdainful expression: she looked like one who would be amiable to few, ill-tempered to most, but true to the death to her husband or her lover.

The hunters were all in their summer clothing, wearing the usual brass-buttoned blue capot with moleskin trousers and calico shirts. Wide-awakes, or cloth caps with peaks, were the favourite head coverings. Gaily embroidered saddle-cloths and belts were evidently preferred to those of a less showy appearance; red, white, and blue beading on a black cloth ground seemed to form the most general arrangement.

James Carnegie, Earl of Southesk

Foot Race

Proposed a race for a flannel shirt. Fifteen champions stripped ready to start. Although among my halfbreeds were several splendid runners, I could not persuade any of them to enter the lists. Felix, however, whom I pressed very hard to contend for the prize, remonstrated, saying that he was an old married man with five children, and that it was unreasonable of me to ask him to run; finally he exclaimed, "I will not run unless you order me, in which case, of course, I cannot help myself." I replied, "I order you to run." With a shrug of his shoulders and a glance of satisfaction he could hardly conceal, he walked to the starting post. The distance was 200 yards down a gentle slope, and thence up a more rapidly rising ground. Felix and the fifteen youths made an excellent start. The race was well contested for the first 120 yards, but as they ascended the rising ground Felix, who was slightly in the rear when in the valley, began to gain at every stride, passed the three foremost, and came in the winner by three yards, and carried off the red flannel shirt.

John Palliser

Halfbreed traders with members of the Boundary Commission, c.1873. Photo by: Royal Engineers

Famine

During this period the only civilized person who visited us was Mr. Tait, a halfbreed in the Company's service at Carlton, who came over in a dog cariole to collect furs from the Indians in our neighbourhood. He brought us a few cakes and potatoes, luxuries we had not tasted for many weeks. From him we learnt that almost everywhere there had been great scarcity of food. At the fort at Egg Lake the people had been obliged to boil down buffalo hides for subsistence. Two men sent over to the nearest fort, Touchwood Hills, for succour, arrived almost dead with famine; but there they found the inmates at the last extremity and unable to afford them any assistance. At Fort La Corne the men had been half-starved for a long time: and even at Carlton the hunters were sent out so scantily provided that they were driven to eating their dogs on the way. We considered ourselves very fortunate in having escaped so well from the general dearth.

The buffalo have receded so far from the forts, and the quantity of whitefish from the lakes, one of the principal sources of supply, has decreased so greatly that now a winter rarely passes without serious suffering from want of food. This deficiency has become so urgent that the Hudson's Bay Company contemplate the immediate establishment of extensive farms in the Saskatchewan district, which is so admirably adapted for agricultural and grazing purposes.

The days when it was possible to live in plenty by the gun and net alone have already gone by on the North Saskatchewan.

Milton and Cheadle

Christmas Dinner

At the head, before Mr. Harriett, was a large dish of boiled buffalo hump; at the foot smoked a boiled buffalo calf. Start not, gentle reader, the calf is very small, and is taken from the cow by the caesarean operation long before it attains its full growth. This, boiled whole, is one of the most esteemed dishes amongst the epicures of the Interior. My pleasing duty was to help a dish of mouffle, or dried moose nose; the gentleman on my left distributed, with graceful impartiality, the whitefish, delicately browned in buffalo marrow. The worthy priest helped the buffalo tongue, whilst Mr. Rundell cut up the beavers' tails. Nor was the other gentleman left unemployed, as all his spare time was occupied in dissecting a roast wild goose. The centre of the table was graced with piles of potatoes, turnips, and bread conveniently placed, so that each could help himself without interrupting the labours of his companions. Such was our jolly Christmas dinner at Edmonton; and long will it remain in my memory. . . .

In the evening the hall was prepared for the dance to which Mr. Harriett had invited all the inmates of the fort, and was early filled by the gaily dressed guests. Indians whose chief ornament consisted in the paint on their faces, voyageurs with bright sashes and neatly ornamented moccasins, halfbreeds glittering in every ornament they could lay their hands on; whether civilized or savage, all were laughing and jabbering in as many different languages as there were styles of dress. English, however, was little used, as none could speak it but those who sat at the dinner table. The dancing was most picturesque and almost all joined in it. Occasionally I, among the rest, led out a young Cree squaw who sported enough beads round her neck to have made a pedlar's fortune and, having led her into the centre of the room, I danced round her with all the agility I was capable of exhibiting to some highland reel tune which the fiddler played with great vigour, whilst my partner with grave face kept jumping up and down, both feet off the ground at once, as only an Indian can dance.

Paul Kane

Fort Edmonton from point below the Wesleyan Mission, 1871. Photo by: Charles Horetzky

Plum Pudding

The Doctor eclipsed all his former efforts in the way of providing medical comforts by concocting a plum pudding for dinner.... — But how? We had neither bag, suet, nor plums. But we had berry-pemmican — it contained buffalo fat that would do for suet and berries that would do for plums. Only genius could have united plum pudding and berry-pemmican in one mental act. Terry contributed a bag and, when the contribution was inspected rather daintily, he explained that it was the sugar bag, which might be used as there was very little sugar left for it to hold. Pemmican, flour and water, baking soda, sugar and salt were surely sufficient ingredients; as a last touch the Doctor searched the medicine-chest, but in vain, for tincture of ginger to give a flavour, and in default of that suggested chlorodyne; but the Chief promptly negatived the suggestion on the ground that if we ate the pudding the chlorodyne might be required a few hours after.

At 3 p.m. the bag was put in the pot, and dinner was ordered to be at 5. At the appointed hour everything else was ready; the usual *pièce de résistance* of pemmican, flanked for Sunday garnishing by two reindeer tongues. But as we gathered round it was announced that the pudding was a failure; that it would not unite; that buffalo fat was not equal in cohesive power to suet, and that instead of a pudding it would be only boiled pemmican. The Doctor might have been knocked down with a feather; Frank was loud and savage in his lamentations; but the Chief advised "more boiling" as an infallible specific in such cases, and that dinner be proceeded with. The additional half hour acted like a charm. With fear and trembling the Doctor went to the pot; anxious heads bent down with his; tenderly was the bag lifted out and slit; and a joyous shout conveyed the intelligence that it was a success, that at any rate it had the shape of a pudding. Brown, who had been scoffing, was silenced; and the Doctor conquered him completely by helping him to a double portion. How good that pudding was! A teaspoonful of brandy on a sprinkling of sugar made sauce; and there was not one of the party who did not hold out his plate for more.

George Grant

Theatre

My readers will naturally ask how, in a wild country like this, theatrical representations could be given. Nevertheless these plays are of frequent occurrence, and this is how the matter is arranged.

First, a managing committee is formed whose duty it is to make all necessary preparations, and to invite the guests. Invitations are frequently sent to a distance of fifty miles, and thus the guests are sometimes reckoned by hundreds. As these balls sometimes last five or six days, an abundance of provisions must be prepared. It was to a ball of this character that I was invited, and both the play and the ball took place within the fort itself. I arrived at five p.m., and very soon the hall was crowded. On the platform in front of the curtain was seated a halfbreed, a very passable violinist, who played a few military marches followed by different national anthems and ended with the *Marseillaise*, amid the hearty applause of all present. The curtain rose and then began the representation of a rustic scene composed for the occasion and entitled "Hard Times." It would take up too much space and time to give an analysis of the play; suffice it to say that it lasted three hours, the different characters were well sustained throughout, and the hall resounded with merited applause from the spectators. The play ended, a bountiful supper was disposed of, and the play-room cleared for the dance. Here the white guests danced by themselves and after the usual fashion, while the halfbreeds, who formed the largest part of the assembly, retired to another apartment and organized a dance of their own and one more suited to their tastes and habits.

Jean d'Artigue

Interior of Fort Edmonton, 1871. Photo by: Charles Horetzky

Cold

The weather turned intensely cold — far more severe than any we had before experienced. Light showers of snow fell in minute particles — as it were frozen dew — when the sun was shining brightly and the sky without a cloud. Clothed in three or four flannel shirts, one of duffel, and a leather shirt; our hands encased in "mittaines," or large gloves of moose-skin lined with duffel, made without fingers, large enough to admit of being easily doffed on occasion and carried slung by a band round the neck; our feet swathed in bands of duffel, covered by enormous moccasins; and our ears and necks protected by a curtain of fur, we were yet hardly able to keep warm with the most active exercise; and when we stayed to camp, shivered and shook as we essayed to light a fire.

Masses of ice the size of a man's fist formed on Cheadle's beard and moustache — the only ones in the company — from the moisture of the breath freezing as it passed through the hair. The oil froze in the pipes we carried about our persons so that it was necessary to thaw them at the fire before they could be made to draw. The hands could hardly be exposed for a moment, except when close to the fire. A bare finger laid upon iron stuck to it as if glued from the instantaneous freezing of its moisture. The snow melted only close to the fire, which formed a trench for itself in which it slowly sank to the level of the ground. The steam rose in clouds, and in the coldest, clearest weather it almost shrouded the fire from view. The snow was light and powdery and did not melt beneath the warmth of the foot, so that our moccasins were as dry on a journey as if we had walked through sawdust instead of snow. The parchment windows of our little hut were so small and opaque that we could hardly see even to eat by their light alone, and were generally obliged to have the door open; and then, although the room was very small and the fireplace very large, a crust of ice formed over the tea in our tin cups as we sat within a yard of the roaring fire. One effect of the cold was to give a most ravenous appetite for fat. Many a time have we eaten great lumps of hard grease — rancid tallow, used for making candles — without bread or anything to modify it.

Milton and Cheadle

Hot Toddy

Still, despite all the "cheering" properties ascribed to tea and coffee when camping after a hard day, tired, cold, wet, and lonely, I say, give me a good horn of hot rum-and-water in preference to the much loved Congou, or the fragrant decoction from the berry of Mocha. Many will cry out, "What a depraved taste!" All I shall attempt to say in defence of my depravity is that I have tried both during extreme hardship, and rum-and-water sets me up, warms me from my head to my heels, and under its influence I turn into sleep as a hunter only can sleep. Tea, if it can be procured, does not do this, and coffee made from berries, tough and hard as bits of hickory, roasted in a frying pan then pounded up betwixt two stones, tied into the toe of a sock and, lastly, boiled in the pannikin until black and bitter, and in flavour remarkably like to porter mixed with Epsom salts, is, to my palate, not a mixture at all calculated to impart very lively emotions to a tired traveller; but *de gustibus non est disputandum.*

John Keast Lord

Mountains

One solitary gleam of consolation enlivened this weary day — an unexpected, far-distant view of two grand peaks of the Rocky Mountains, over which a thundercloud cast a solemn, leaden shade. It was but an imperfect view, but so marvellous was the contrast between the damp, confined darkness of our track through the dripping fir trees and the sudden freedom of an open sky bounded only by magnificent mountain forms, that for a moment I was quite overwhelmed. Then one of those strange tides of emotion that transcend both control and analysis rushed through me from head to foot — I trembled all over — my limbs lost their strength, I could hardly sit on my horse. He, poor beast, did not share in his rider's excitement — as in a momentary fancy I thought he would — and seemed no happier than before; but, for my own part, all weariness vanished away, and I felt myself ready for any labours that might bring me nearer to so splendid a goal.

James Carnegie, Earl of Southesk

Jasper House, Alberta, 1872. Photo by: Charles Horetzky

Missionaries

There are very few tents about the mission at present, the Indians being in the plains engaged in hunting the buffalo. Mr. Settee speaks English very fluently, the field for his labour is extensive but not at present promising. When conversing with the Crees of the Sandy Hills, many of them expressed a wish to have their children taught by white men, but they did not appear to like the idea of their being taught by a native of a different origin. This is an important point to be observed in the selection of native missionaries. The school, however, appears here, as elsewhere among Indian tribes, to be the only sure ground for establishing the true faith among them. "Teach my children for two or three years, but let me follow the ways of my fathers," said the son of the chief of the Sandy Hills to me. Many expressed a wish that their little ones should know the white man's cunning and learn to cultivate the soil, but they would stipulate to remain themselves still the wild prairie Indians, hunting the buffalo and occasionally tasting the savage excitement of war.

It is a wrong policy to send a Swampy Cree among the Plain Crees, or an Ojibway amongst the Crees, as a teacher and minister of religion. These highly sensitive and jealous people do not willingly accept gifts or favours which involve any recognition of mental superiority in the donor from one not of their own kindred, language, and blood, although he may be of their own race. An Ojibway remains always an Ojibway and a Swampy Cree a Swampy Cree in the eyes of the haughty and independent children of the prairies, and they will never acknowledge or respect them as teachers of the "white man's religion."

Henry Youle Hind

Fashion

The universal passion for dress is strangely illustrated in the western Indian. His ideal of perfection is the English costume of some forty years ago. The tall chimney-pot hat with round narrow brim, the coat with high collar going up over the neck, sleeves tight-fitting, waist narrow. All this is perfection, and the chief who can array himself in this ancient garb struts out of the fort the envy and admiration of all beholders. Sometimes the tall felt chimney-pot is graced by a large feather which has done duty in the turban of a dowager thirty years ago in England. The addition of a little gold tinsel to the coat collar is of considerable consequence, but the presence of a nether garment is not at all requisite to the completeness of the general get-up. For this most ridiculous-looking costume a Blackfoot chief will readily exchange his beautifully-dressed deerskin Indian shirt — embroidered with porcupine quills and ornamented with the raven locks of his enemies — his head-dress of ermine skins, his flowing buffalo robe: a dress in which he looks every inch a savage king for one in which he looks every inch a foolish savage. But the new dress does not long survive — bit by bit it is found unsuited to the wild work which its owner has to perform; and although it never loses the high estimate originally set upon it, nevertheless it is discarded by virtue of the many inconveniences arising out of running buffalo in a tall beaver, or fighting in a tail-coat against Crees.

William Francis Butler

Prayers

They are all very religious, having been converted by the Roman Catholic priests. Frequently, and at stated times, a bell is rung in the camp, and all who are within hearing at once go down on their knees and pray. This well-meant custom had rather a ludicrous effect on us once for, in the evening, when a couple of Indians were holding a cow they had lassoed for us and Beads was busy milking it in spite of its kicks and struggles, the little bell was heard and down popped the Indians on their knees, letting go their hold of the cow without any warning to poor Beads who was, of course, doubled up in a twinkling but without any damage beyond the loss of the milk.

John Palliser

Piegan Indians, Rocky Mountain House, Alberta, 1871. Photo by: Charles Horetzky

Hard Going

From the Clearwater to the Lesser Slave Lake occupied nine days; but the country was so uninteresting, our progress so slow, and the daily course of events so monotonous, that I shall pass over that interval. The intervening country bore a great resemblance to that lying between the head waters of the Ottawa and the southern shores of Hudson's Bay, being hilly, swampy, and densely wooded. The timber is principally spruce, balsam, poplar and birch; and wherever the land has any tendency to be level, it is almost invariably swampy and covered with cranberries and blackberries. For nearly the entire distance, the trail was hardly discernible; our animals mired at every swamp we came to, and those were by no means of rare occurrence, the botanist having counted twenty-seven separate and distinct ones during the course of one day's travel. We seemed during those nine days to have experienced all the misfortunes incidental to pack-train travelling. One of our horses was impaled on a sharp stump, and nearly bled to death; another, worn by fatigue, ultimately became a prey to the wolves; our provisions got materially damaged; and, to crown all, the weather, which had been so propitious during our journey over the plains, seemed now bent on making us pay for former benefits, and enlivened us with continued storms of rain and wind, which occasionally alternated to sleet and snow. Upon the whole, we had a remarkable time of it, and were not sorry to catch the first glimpse of the Lake, which we reached on the afternoon of the 20th.

Charles Horetzky

Campfire

We encamped early, making for the first time what is called a regular winter encampment. This is only made where the snow is so deep that it cannot be removed so as to reach the ground. The depth to which the snow attains can be calculated by the stumps of the trees cut off at its former level for previous campfires; some of these were twelve or fifteen feet above us at the present time, and the snow was nine or ten feet deep under us. Some of the old voyageurs amused themselves by telling the new hands, or *mangeurs du lard*, that the Indians in those parts were giants from thirty to forty feet high, and that accounted for the trees being cut off at such an unusual height.

It is necessary to walk repeatedly with snowshoes over the place chosen for the encampment until it is sufficiently beaten down to

bear a man without sinking on its surface. Five or six logs of green timber from eighteen to twenty feet long are laid down close together, in parallel lines, so as to form a platform. The fire of dry wood is then kindled on it, and pine branches are spread on each side on which the party, wrapped in their blankets, lie down with their feet towards the fire. The parallel logs rarely burn through in one night, but the dropping coal and heat form a deep chasm immediately under the fire, into which the logs are prevented from falling by their length.

Paul Kane

Feast

February 27th — After starting this morning we fell on a creek flowing to the east, and as the timber is quite burnt off this part of the country we got a fine view which included a few distant peaks of the Rocky Mountains. The fallen trees rendered walking very laborious, however, as our snowshoes frequently caught in the knots and made us fall, which was very trying to our tempers, already much soured by starvation. At noon we arrived at a little swampy valley where the snow was trodden down as if by the tracks of a large band of buffalo. However, Tekarra after looking around said it was only the place where three moose-deers had been feeding all winter, and with wonderful quickness he picked out their most recent tracks, and told us to go on steadily and only to halt if he fired three shots, which was to be a sign he had killed one of them. We had only gone a mile when we heard a shot, and immediately after two others. This at once banished our fatigue, and regardless of the deep snow and fallen timber we made off in the direction of the firing. Here we found Tekarra busy cutting up a fine three-year-old moose, which was the youngest of two he had seen. We at once made a fire by the carcass, which lay among fallen timber where the snow was about four feet deep. Our appetite was tremendous so that, although the flesh of the animal was so lean that at other times we would not have eaten it, we continued cooking, eating, and sleeping the remainder of that day and the whole of the next, by which time there was little left of the moose but the coarser parts of the meat. Our three dogs also, who had eaten nothing but the bones of the grouse and our cast-off moccasins since leaving Jasper House, enjoyed themselves to the full; indeed both the dogs and masters conducted themselves more like wolves than was altogether seemly, excepting under such circumstances.

John Palliser

Members of Horetzky's survey party in the Athabasca Valley, Alberta, 1872. Photo by: Charles Horetzky

Troops on the way to Humboldt, Saskatchewan, North-west Rebellion, 1885. Photo by: O.B. Buell

June 8th — Travelled on rather fast; at noon found a lost horse, evidently must have belonged to the Sarcees. Petope claimed the horse, according to prairie law, and having seen him first; I resisted the claim, would not allow any one to have the horse. Petope left, in consequence, in a rage. I allowed him to go, but afterwards sent after him when he was cool, and speechified him into acquiescence of my conduct, explaining to him the difference between prairie law, which was to seize all you could, and the Queen's law, which was to endeavour to do your best always to restore property to its rightful owner.

John Palliser

Montreal Garrison Artillery, Pie-à-Pot and braves, North-west Rebellion, 1885. Photo by: O.B. Buell

We occasionally met sensational rumours regarding alleged acts of violence on the part of the Indians, but further inquiry always proved these rumours to be baseless. Even when sorely pressed by hunger, and when pained by the sight of friends suffering from starvation, they displayed the utmost patience and endurance, and made no attempt to procure relief by violence. Throughout the whole country the white settlers are undisturbed by any anxiety about them; and the natural course of events must tend to make the whites every year more and more secure against any likelihood of trouble from this quarter.

Rev. Daniel Gordon

Members of Louis Riel's council in Regina after the North-west Rebellion, 1885. Photo by: O.B. Buell

The most curious anomaly among the race of man, the red man of America, is passing away beneath our eyes into the infinite solitude. The possession of the same noble qualities which we affect to reverence among our nations makes us kill him. If he would be as the African or the Asiatic it would be all right for him; if he would be our slave he might live, but as he won't be that, won't toil and delve and hew for us, and will persist in hunting, fishing, and roaming over the beautiful prairie land which the Great Spirit gave him; in a word, since he will be free — we kill him.

William Francis Butler

PART III
B.C. INTERIOR

Dignity

At 8:30 a.m., as breakfast was getting ready, a distinguished visitor appeared, an old stately-looking Indian, a chief.... He came with only one attendant; but two or three canoes made their appearance about the same time, with other Indians, squaws, and papooses who squatted in groups on the banks at respectful distances. The old Indian came up with a "B'jou, B'jou," shook hands all round, and then drawing himself up — knife in one hand, big pipe in the other, the emblems of war and peace — commenced a long harangue. We didn't understand a word; but one of the men roughly interpreted, and the speaker's gestures were so expressive that the drift of his meaning could be easily followed. Pointing with outstretched arms north, south, east and west, he told us that all the land had been his people's, and that he now, in their name, asked for some return for our passage through it. The aim of all the eloquence was simply a breakfast; but the bearing and speech were those of a born orator. He had good straight features, a large Roman nose, square chin, and, as he stood over six feet in his moccasins, his presence was most commanding. One great secret of impressive gesticulation — the free play of the arm from the shoulder, instead of the cramped motion from the elbow — he certainly knew. It was astonishing with what dignity and force long, rolling, musical sentences poured from the lips of one who would be carelessly classed by most people as a savage to whose views no regard should be paid. When ended, he took a seat on a hillock with the dignity natural to every real Indian, and began to smoke in perfect silence. He had said his say, and it was our turn now. Without answering his speech, which we could only have done in a style far inferior to his, the Chief proposed that he should have some breakfast. To show due respect to so great an O-ghe-mah, a newspaper was spread before him as a tablecloth, and a plate of fried pork placed on it, with a huge "slapjack" or thick pancake made of flour and fat, one-sixth of which was as much as any white man's stomach could digest. A large pannikin of tea, a beverage the Indians are immoderately fond of, was also brought and, by signs, he was invited to "fall to." For some moments he made no movement, either from offended pride or expectation that we would join him or, more likely, only to show a gentlemanly indifference to the food. But the fat pork and the fragrant tea were irresistible. Many a great man's dignity has been overcome by less. After he had eaten about half, he summoned his attendant to sit beside him and eat, and to him, too, a pannikin of tea was brought. We then told the old man that we had heard his words; that we were travellers carrying only enough food for ourselves, but that we would bring his views to the notice of the Government, and that his tribe would certainly receive justice, as it was the desire of our Great Mother the Queen that all her children — red as well as white — should be well cared for. He at once assented, though whether he would have done so with equal blandness had we given him no breakfast is questionable.

George Grant

Baptiste and the Salmon Chief of the Schweilp Indians at Fort Colville, Washington, 1860-61. Photo by: Royal Engineers

Outfitted

A few words here as to our personal equipment may be permitted. For trips such as these I always wore a shooting jacket with as many pockets as possible; strong corduroy trousers, tied under the knee after the fashion of English navvies to take the drag off it when they are wet; and an old uniform cap, which I always found had a capital effect upon Indians, inspiring them with an idea of the wearer's exalted position as a "Hyas Tyee," or great chief. Slung over my shoulder I carried an aneroid which, with a spy-glass, completed my equipment. Dr. Campbell carried the gun on this occasion, as I had a chronometer in my pocket, which it was of the greatest importance not to disturb, and I therefore did not shoot. My spare things, packed in a small valise, consisted of a clean flannel shirt, six or eight pairs of socks, a Hudson's Bay capot (a sort of blue frock-coat, made with a hood to it) — upon the cuffs of which a lieutenant's gold lace was put to add to the effect, and which was worn before the natives upon all particularly important occasions — and a coat and trousers made of blue blanket, which I put on as soon as we camped at night, and in which I always slept. As to provisions, all we ever carried was a side or two of bacon, four or five bags of flour — the quantity depending upon the time that was likely to elapse before fresh stores could be reached — plenty of tea and coffee, and a bottle of brandy in case of accidents.

R.C. Mayne

An Ordinary Day

December 12th — The winter is still mild and open, playing fast and loose; we have it pretty cold for a few days, go to bed with six or seven inches of snow on the ground and in the morning wake up to find it all disappeared like magic and a drizzling rain coming down instead. This is very bad for sleigh travelling, as we are liable to get caught by one of these sudden thaws when far away from the barracks and then have either to wait for another fall of snow or ride the horses home and leave the sleigh to take care of itself. I will give you an example of the way one day is passed, which you can multiply by the number of days in the winter and have a good idea of how we manage to kill time: I generally get up at about eight and dressing and breakfast wile away the hours till half past nine, then writing and business till two or half past two when I always go out either for a walk or in the sleigh returning about five; we dine at six and after dinner read or have a game of back-gammon or rubber of whist till ten or eleven o'clock, then to bed to go through the same course on the morrow. We have seen nothing of our neighbours, the American volunteers, but we occasionally hear of their doings. The officers and men had a fight amongst themselves the other day, what they call a "free fight", everyone against his neighbour, in which considerable damage was done to the faces and prominent features of the belligerents. A small Indian fight about a couple of miles from this in which one Indian was nearly killed and the white men obliged to make a run for it, and a melancholy accident in which a canoe was upset in a rapid and two men drowned, are the only events that have happened lately.

December 24th — Our cook having cleverly contrived to boil up his pipe and tobacco with the soup, we spent a rather cheerless Christmas Eve and everyone went to bed at an early hour, with vastly unpleasant sensation.

Charles Wilson

John Keast Lord, naturalist to the North American Boundary Commission, at Fort Colville, Washington, 1860-61. Photo by: Royal Engineers

Windstorm

Sappers clearing the International Boundary line on Moyie River, B.C., 1860-61. Photo by: Royal Engineers

February 20th — Last night a heavy gale got up and made us all feel very uncomfortable. I could not sleep for a long time. The night was pitch dark and as I lay on the ground, with my buffalo robe round me, I could hear the thundering of the trees as they were blown down all round us. In the morning we heard the sad news that a tree had fallen on one of the tents at a camp about eight miles off and killed one of the men; there were nine in the tent but by a perfect miracle all escaped but one. The gale kept blowing the whole day with great violence and we had to go and hold an inquest on the body; so, mounting our horses, off we went and a rather hazardous journey it was, trees falling all round us like ninepins and sometimes the tops, broken clean off, would come rattling down close beside us, obliging us, as one of our American axemen observed, to keep "our eyes pretty considerably skinned," which meaneth to keep our eyes open. We however got through all right. The poor man, who was an axeman and had lately joined us, must have been killed instantaneously; the man sleeping next to him had a wonderful escape, the tree actually grazing him. We got back again to our own camp about six when the wind began to fall and before we turned in nearly died away, so we went to sleep in peace with feeling of great satisfaction at not having been squashed during the day. This is the second man we have lost by the falling of trees within three weeks, which has cast a gloom over the whole party.

Charles Wilson

Cache

A small amount of provisons for dogs and men was left at the cache for those who were to return this way to Fort George. From our camp, which was on an island at the foot of the first canyon, we distinctly heard the sound of chopping on the opposite bank just as we were turning in, but no one could be persuaded away from the warm camp to solve any such mystery as this, although every one agreed there was something strange about it, no tracks having been seen; and if it were Indians, they would have been round our fire ere this. Yet there were the distinct and separate blows of the axe, and the crash of the falling tree on the river bank not two hundred yards from us, and the most careful search the following morning failed to show that any such thing had taken place. So much for the power of imagination. The great cold of last week had abated since the snowstorm, and we managed to keep very snug in camp and warm at night by sleeping two together, and pretty close at that.

Charles Hanington

Caching provisions at the Forks of the North Thompson River, B.C., 1871. Photo by: Benjamin Baltzly

Kaye's Ranch, Thompson River, B.C., c.1865. Photo by: Charles Gentile

Spokane Indians at Fort Colville, Washington, 1860-61. Photo by: Royal Engineers

Referring to your Lordship's circular of the 30th of November, transmitting a copy of the letter from Professor Huxley, suggesting that photographs might be collected from the various colonies, having much ethnological value as illustrating the peculiarities of the different races within the British possessions. I have endeavoured to give effect to your Lordship's desire to further this design. But it has been found impracticable to obtain photographs of the character required. I am informed that no Indians here will consent to be photographed in a state of nudity, although reward has been offered. It is believed that they have a superstitious dread of some hidden purpose which they do not understand, and it would be impossible to explain to them the scientific object of the proceeding.

Anthony Musgrave

Opportunities

Respectable females, neither afraid nor ashamed to work as domestic servants, are greatly in demand. Strong and active young women qualified to serve as efficient cooks and housemaids would have no difficulty in obtaining from £4 to £5 per month and board. So much is the want of this class felt that, if 500 girls of good character and industrious habits could be sent out in detachments of fifty in each vessel and at intervals of a month, they would be absorbed almost immediately on their arrival. But the presence of this sex is as urgently required on social and moral grounds. There are many well-disposed single men prospering in the various trades and professions who are anxious to adopt the country as their home. But the scope for selecting wives is so limited that they feel compelled to go to California in search of their interesting object, and not unfrequently are they tempted to remain on American soil — their industry as producers and expenditure as consumers being lost to the colonies. There is no territory on the globe presenting to unmarried virtuous females such opportunities of entering that state upon which every right-minded woman cannot but look with approval.

Matthew Macfie

Schweilp woman and child at Fort Colville, Washington, 1860-61. Photo by: Royal Engineers

Miss Irving and Miss Brown on the Cariboo Road near Yale, B.C., 1868. Photo by: Frederick Dally

Graves

Near our encampment there was a native cemetery, the neat little tombs being surrounded by pickets. We were surprised, however, to see a wooden cross placed at the head of each grave, the result of a recent visit of some Catholic priests; but, as a practical illustration of the value of such conversions, we found on a neighbouring tree a number of offerings to one of the departed spirits and a basket of provisions for its voyage to the next world. If the Indians had any definite idea at all of the cross they put it merely on the same footing as their other medicines or charms.

George Simpson

Funeral Rites

When a chief dies, of course, according to the redskin creed, he will require in the next world — the happy hunting grounds to which he has gone — all the luxuries and necessaries his good fortune enabled him to enjoy in this: so it generally happens that two or three slaves (male and female), two or three horses, and two or three dogs are shot, and laid on or in the earth where rest the remains of the departed. But I have always observed that very old slaves and very ancient canine and equine quadrupeds are deemed by the sorrowing relatives quite good enough to send on such a hazardous journey — a wise economy, worthy of a better cause.

John Keast Lord

In the interior of New Caledonia, which is east of Vancouver Island and north of the Columbia, among the tribe called Taw-wa-tins, who are also Babines, and also among other tribes in their neighbourhood, the custom prevails of burning the bodies, with circumstances of peculiar barbarity to the widows of the deceased. The dead body of the husband is laid naked upon a large heap of resinous wood; his wife is then placed upon the body and covered over with a skin; the pile is then lighted and the poor woman is compelled to remain until she is nearly suffocated, when she is allowed to descend as best she can through the smoke and flames. No sooner, however, does she reach the ground than she is expected to prevent the body from becoming distorted by the action of the fire on the muscles and sinews; and whenever such an event takes place she must, with her bare hands, restore the burn-ing corpse to its proper position, her person being the whole time exposed to the scorching effects of the intense heat. Should she fail in the due performance of this indispensable rite from weakness or the intensity of her pain, she is held up by somone until the body is consumed. A continual singing and beating of drums is kept up throughout the ceremony, which drowns her cries. Afterwards she must collect the unconsumed pieces of bone and ashes and put them into a bag made for the purpose, which she has to carry on her back for three years remaining for the time a slave to her husband's relations and being neither allowed to wash nor comb herself for the whole time so that she soon becomes a most disgusting object. At the expiration of the three years a feast is given by her tormentors, who invite all the friends and relations of her and themselves. At the commencement they deposit with great ceremony the remains of the burnt dead in a box, which they affix to the top of a high pole, and dance around it. The widow is then stripped naked and smeared from head to foot with fish oil, over which one of the bystanders throws a quantity of swan's down, covering her entire person. She is then obliged to dance with the others. After all this is over she is free to marry again, if she has the inclination, and courage enough to venture on a second risk of being roasted alive and the subsequent horrors.

It has often happened that a widow who has married a second husband, in the hope perhaps of not outliving him, committed suicide in the event of her second husband's death rather than undergo a second ordeal. I was unable to learn any explanation of the motive for these cruel rites and can only account for them in the natural selfishness, laziness, and cruelty of the Indians, who probably hope by these means to render their wives more attentive to their personal ease and comfort; whilst, at the same time, it secures them from assassination either by a jealous or an errant spouse.

Paul Kane

Grave of Couteaux chief near Lytton, B.C., 1867. Photo by: Frederick Dally

Ox team at Clinton, Cariboo Road, B.C., 1868. Photo by: Frederick Dally

We arrived about four o'clock in the afternoon and immediately ordered the best dinner they could give us. The house was kept by a Frenchman who excelled himself on this occasion and provided a meal which to us, who had not eaten anything deserving the name of a dinner for at least eighteen months, appeared perfection. The champagne, however, and sundry drinks with fraternizing miners caused us to wake with most tremendous headaches next morning. Some of the visitors to the bar amused us greatly. One tall Yankee, considerably intoxicated, was possessed with the idea that he was Lord Nelson and, associating the great admiral in some way with cucumbers, ate several in succession to prove his identity.

Milton and Cheadle

Siseanjute (centre), Chief of the Bonaparte Indians, and band members at Lytton, B.C., c.1867. Photo by: Frederick Dally   101

Fisherman

Among other materials wherewith to make a fly, feathers were indispensable. Shouldering my gun, I strode off to look for a "white flesher," alias ruffed grouse; soon stirred one up, bagged him, hauled out his glossy bottle-green frill; selected some feathers which I thought would turn a decent hackle, picked out a couple of brighter ones for wings, some red wool from my blanket for dubbing, and with these materials I tied a fly. Not the slightest resemblance, fancied or real, did it bear to anything ever created, but still it was a fly, and, as I flattered myself, a great achievement. A line was made from some ends of cord; then cutting a young larch, I made my tackle fast to the end, and thus equipped sallied to the stream.

My first attempt in the swift scour was a lamentable failure. Warily I threw my newly created monster well across the stream, and, according to the most approved method, let it slowly wash towards me, conveying to the rod and line a delicate and tempting tremble; not a rise, not a nibble; my hopes wavered, and I began to think these trout wiser than I had given them credit for. I tried the pool as a last chance; so, leaning over the rock, I let my tempter drop into the water; it made a splash like throwing in a stone; but imagine my delight, ye lovers of the gentle art, when a tremendous jerk told me I had one hooked and struggling to get free! Depending on the strength of my tackle, I flung him out on the bank; and admitting all that may be said against me as being barbarous and cruel, I confess to standing over the dying fish, and admiring his brilliant colour, handsome shape, fair proportion — and, last though not least, contemplated eating him!

John Keast Lord

Salmon Run

One day I went down to the Kettle Falls to see the Indians catching salmon. The falls are most beautiful, the whole river falling over a ledge of quartz into a sort of cauldron in which the water bubbles and boils in a most remarkable manner from which the falls takes its name. The fishery, however, is the great sight and certainly is the most wonderful one I ever saw. The salmon arrive at the foot of the falls in great numbers and proceed to leap them; all day long you see one continual stream of fish in the air, many of them clear the whole at a single leap, others not so lucky just get halfway and you see them quivering for a few seconds in the perpendicular water when down they come and are carried into an eddy just at your feet, where you can see them resting themselves for another trial. The Indian way of catching them is very ingenious. They hang a basket made of willow or crab apple over the rock at the side of the falls, the salmon in jumping strike their noses against the top part and fall into the basket below; they catch from 700 to 1,000 salmon a day in this manner which are equally divided amongst them in the evening by one of the chiefs. The most curious sight is to see them empty the basket; two men strip and jump into it armed with wooden bludgeons with which they knock the salmon on the head and then pass them on to others on shore; it is rather an awkward situation in this same basket as part of the fall, though not the full force of it, runs right over their heads nearly drowning them whilst what with the weight of the fish and the rush of the water the frail basket rocks about in anything but a pleasant manner.

Charles Wilson

Rescue

The place where the horse had slipped and struggled was easily found, for the bark torn off the recumbent trunks marked the course of his headlong descent. The place from which he fell was about 120 or 130 feet above the river, and the last 30 or 40 feet of this a perpendicular face of rock. Cheadle crept down and looked over the edge, and on a little flat space below saw Bucephalus, astride of a large tree, lengthwise. The tree was propped up by others horizontally at such a height that the animal's legs hung down on each side without touching the ground. The two then descended, expecting to find him mortally injured but, to their astonishment, he appeared quite comfortable in his novel position. The packs were taken off and Cheadle, by a vigorous lift — Mr. O'B. declining the suggestion that he should haul at the tail, on the ground of the dangerous nature of the service — rolled the horse from his perch.

Milton and Cheadle

Cascade on Garnet Creek, B.C., 1871. Photo by: Benjamin Baltzly

103

Gathering of "the greatest Indian Chiefs of British Columbia" at New Westminster, B.C., 1867. Photo by: Frederick Dally

When paying off the men we had occasion to notice what we had observed on previous occasions, a great reluctance on their part to tell their names, a reluctance amounting almost to a superstitious dread. When asked their names they usually request some companion to reply for them; and even in referring to each other, they will often use a roundabout description rather than the appropriate name. A woman in speaking of her husband will sometimes point to her son and refer to her husband as "that boy's father" rather than mention his name. One of our men, Jim, was so called by us because we could not ascertain his correct name, and we required some way by which to distinguish him from the others.

Rev. Daniel Gordon

104

Tranquille Mills, Kamloops Lake, B.C., 1871. Photo by: Benjamin Baltzly

Rapid of the Dead

We camped at night below the "Dalle des Morts," or the Rapid of the Dead, so called from the following circumstance. About twenty-five or thirty years ago, an Iroquois, a halfbreed, and a French Canadian, having charge of a boat, had to descend this frightful rapid. Fearful of running it they affixed a long line to the bow, and being themselves on the shore, they attempted to lower her gradually by means of it down the foaming torrent. The boat took a sheer and ran outside of a rock, and all their efforts to get her back or reach the rock themselves through the boiling surge were unavailing. The rope, chafing on the sharp edge of the rock, soon broke, and she dashed down amongst the whirling eddies and broke to pieces with their whole stock of provisions on board.

They then continued to follow on foot along the rugged and difficult banks of the river without food, guns, or ammunition; nor had they been able to save even a blanket to protect them from the inclement weather. At night they encamped in a shivering and famishing condition, not having been able to surmount more than three miles of the obstacles that obstructed their passage at every step along the banks. The next day they proceeded with no better success. They well knew that if they constructed a raft it would not live an hour in this part of the Columbia River, owing to the quick succession of rapids that here beset the navigation. In this starving condition they continued their slow progress till the third day when the halfbreed, fearing his companions would kill him for their food, left them and was never after heard of, falling in all probability a prey to the wolves. The other two lay down and the Iroquois, watching his opportunity, got up at night and beat his companion's brains out with a stick, and going to work in a methodical manner, after first satisfying his craving hunger with a portion of the body, cut the remainder into thin slices and dried them in the sun, after the manner in which buffalo meat is prepared. Here he remained three days drying his meat, which he made into a pack, and continued his journey with it down the river bank until he came to the commencement of the Upper Lake, where he made a raft on which he placed his dried meat and covered it over with pine bark, seating himself upon it, and paddling down the lake.

He had not proceeded very far before he met a canoe which had been sent from one of the forts below on the Spokane River in quest of them, owing to their long absence. The newcomers immediately inquired what had become of his two companions; he replied that they had deserted him, giving at the same time an account of the loss of the boat. They took him on board their canoe, and one of the men seeing the bark on the raft and desirous of getting it to place under him in the canoe, the Iroquois shoved off the raft, with evident signs of confusion, on which the man, who noticed his embarrassment, paddled up to it and, lifting the bark, discovered the dried meat beneath it, among which was a human foot. He was asked how he had obtained the dried meat and replied that he had killed a wolf swimming across the river.

The foot with the meat was slyly deposited in a bag belonging to one of the men, but not without the act being perceived by the murderer who, while they were asleep during the night, threw the bag and its contents into the river. Appearing not to notice its loss they went on to Fort Spokane and delivered him up to Mr. McMullan, the person in charge, detailing particulars. The Indian was shortly afterwards sent to a distant post in New Caledonia both as a punishment and also in order to get rid of him, as no voyageur will willingly associate with anyone known to have eaten human flesh.

Paul Kane

Spence's Bridge, Thompson River, B.C., 1865. Photo by: Charles Gentile

"Teamsters breakfasting", Cariboo Road, B.C., 1871.
Photo by: Benjamin Baltzly

El Dorado

The miner has ever got his dream of an El Dorado fresh and sanguine. No disaster, no repeated failure will discourage him. His golden paradise is always "away up" in some half-inaccessible spot in a wilderness of mountains. Nothing daunts him in this wild search of his. Mountains, rivers, canyons are the enemies he is constantly wrestling with. Nature has locked her treasures of gold and silver in deep mountain caverns, as though she would keep them from the daring men who strive to rob her. But she cannot save them. When one sees this wonderful labour, this delving into the bowels of rock and shingle, this turning and twisting of river channel, and sluicing and dredging and blasting going on in these strange out-of-the-way places, the thought occurs, if but the tenth part of this toil were expended by these men in the ordinary avocations of life, they would all be rich or comfortable. The miner cannot settle down — at least for a long time — the life has a strange fascination for him; he will tell you that for one haul he has drawn twenty blanks; he will tell you that he has lost more money in one night at "faro" or "poker" than would suffice to have kept him decently for five years; he will tell you that he has frequently to put two dollars into the ground in order to dig one dollar out of it, and yet he cannot give up the wild, free life. He is emphatically a queer genius; and no matter what his country, his characteristics are the same. It would be impossible to discipline him, yet I think that, were he amenable to even a semblance of restraint and command, 40,000 miners might conquer a continent.

His knowledge of words is peculiar; he has a thousand phrases of his own which it would be needless to follow him into. "Don't prevaricate, sir!" thundered a British Columbian judge to a witness from the mines, "Don't prevaricate, sir!" "Can't help it, judge," answered the miner. "Ever since I got a kick in the mouth from a mule that knocked my teeth out, I prevaricate a good deal."

William Francis Butler

108

The Happy Home Group, Williams Creek, Cariboo, B.C., c.1867. Photo by: Frederick Dally

British Columbia

It is hard to believe that this dependency will be fully peopled, or that its natural capabilities will render it a desirable home for Britons. It wants fine land; it wants prairie; it wants everything except snow, sleet, and rain. . . . When the intending emigrant hears of the mellow Italian softness of the climate, the balmy fragrance of the atmosphere, the serenity of the sky; that the mere upturning of the plough is all that is needful to convert the whole territory into a fruitful garden, let him not believe one word of it; it is all untrue. British Columbia is a miserable country, neither adapted for cattle nor suited for cereals. To the bold and intrepid who desire a wandering and restless life, who believe in the chances of getting rich by the lucky acquisition of gold, these regions offer certain inducements; but to the industrious, prudent, orderly, and virtuous man, all would be wretchedness.

Duncan MacDonald

Petticoat

We returned to our old camping place, on nearing which we saw something we could not make out. "It is", "no, it can't be", such were the expressions; we put our horses to the gallop and, yes, there it was as large as life, in all the grandeur of the most expensive crinoline, a "petticoat in the wilderness"! We could scarcely believe our eyes but yet it was true. This enterprising woman (English, bye the bye) had travelled on horseback over the mountains, through forest and plain, fording the mountain torrents and exposed to all the changes of the weather, and was on her way to set up an inn at Rock Creek, the first white woman who had ever penetrated into these wilds; she was accompanied by her husband, a fine-looking Englishman, and on the backs of sundry mules were packed all the household "fixings" for the future benefit of houseless wanderers in the valley of Nehoialpitku. Success attend her endeavours for she is worthy of it!

Charles Wilson

Settling Down

Most of the inhabitants have been miners and go into other business when their coin runs short. The hotel is kept by Brown and Gillis, who do things in first-class style and charge $3.50 per diem for doing it. Drinks, beer or otherwise, 25 cents per glass, very small glasses. Gillis is a native of P.E. Island and a good fellow he is. As Jarvis is also a P.E. Islander and I a Blue nose, we are great friends of Gillis. The butcher in this town is also from the Lower Provinces, being a Haligonian; his brother is organist in one of our churches there and poor Mike (Hagarty) has gone into the meat business having failed in the mines.

There are several stores here, Read's, Girod's and Kuong Lee's being the most important. Read is a capital fellow and keeps a lot of good cigars for his own and friends' use. Girod is a Frenchman and hot after money. Kuong Lee, the Chinese firm, do a very large business in all sorts of goods; they have on hand a lot of *green ginger* and several kinds of fruit which I had never seen before but which I like exceedingly. Like the other merchants, they are very good at "setting it out" for their customers.

Charles Hanington

Liberty

We were greatly amused at breakfast this morning; everybody feeds together and Haig was situated next to a particularly dirty-looking man who was very offensive to his organs of scent, not having indulged in the luxury of water for many days; a waiter who perceived his annoyance pointed with a broad grin to the end of the room where a scroll of paper with "Liberty" in large letters on it was placed. I was seated opposite to a regular Yankee who used his knife and fork something like a Chinaman does his chopsticks, shoving his knife half way down his throat so that in fear of seeing the knife protrude at the back of his neck and unable to contain myself, I rushed out of the room nearly choking with laughter.

Charles Wilson

Richfield, Cariboo, B.C., c.1868. Photo by: Frederick Dally

Barkerville, Cariboo, B.C., c.1867. Photo by: Frederick Dally

Grouse Creek, Cariboo, B.C., c.1867. Photo by: Frederick Dally

113

Justice

We met Chief Justice Begbie, another name held in profound respect by the miners, Siwashes, and all others among whom he has dealt out justice. Judge Lynch has never been required in British Columbia because Chief Justice Begbie did his duty and maintained the dignity of his Court as effectually as if it had been held in Old Westminster. It is a grand sight to a rightly constituted mind when two or three policemen scatter a street mob. It must have been a grander to see a British judge backed by one or two constables maintaining order at the gold mines among the tag-rag and bob-tail, the rough and tumble, fever-heated classes of miners, gamblers, claim "jumpers" and cutthroats who congregate at such places.... In British Columbia the difficulties in the way of preserving order were greatest, yet the laws have always been respected and enforced, and two or three constables proved sufficient for every emergency. The results have been simply marvellous. *The Times* Cariboo correspondent could write in 1862: "As to security of life I consider it just as safe here as in England." Every week for the last nine years the mail coach has carried a box or boxes of gold dust from Cariboo with no defender but "Steve" or his partner; and though running through a country roamed over by the lawless of every nation, where ambuscades could be planned at every turn, where for long stretches there is neither house nor shanty, it has never been plundered nor even attacked.

George Grant

As may be supposed, the state of society is low in the extreme, and life and property are far from secure. Night and day bands of murderous-looking ruffians prowl about and commit the most atrocious robberies. Indeed no accounts of the discomfort and crimes encountered at the gold fields, however exaggerated, can come near the reality. No man thinks of moving from his tent, by night or by day, without every barrel of his revolver charged and ready for use. At the British Columbian mines, as at all others, the miner dare not lie down at night without his deadly weapon at his side and a companion on the watch to guard him from murder and robbery. Thus they work, and watch, and sleep, and live, in constant dread of death. Some have attached to their treasury box dogs of the fiercest kind to whom human blood is more than palatable. At the darkest hour of night the agonizing shriek and the muffled cry is heard of some poor wretch who is gagged or murdered. But you dare not interfere unless you desire to be yourself shot and to have your tent sacked. Even in the broad light of day, from hiding places in the clefts of the rocks, from the eternal snows of the Rocky Mountains, with no witness but the all-seeing eye of God, have ascended many a cry from lips which never opened more.

Duncan MacDonald

Gold Fever

A digger goes into the office of a broker, where he is requested to turn out his nuggets and dust upon a large sheet of paper which has been carefully punctured so as to allow the finer particles of the dust to fall through upon a second sheet immediately under the first one; then our honest broker begins to shake and shuffle about the glittering metal with the view, as he tells his verdant victim, of preparing the mass for the next skilful trick of the "magnet", with which he rouses and tosses again and again the nuggets and dust; then, having puffed and blown enough, he, in his own simple offhanded manner, empties the lot into a scale and counts in the most scientific and rapid manner: "Eight and six is ten, ten and two is eleven, eleven and seven is thirteen; thirteen ounces, two penny weights and a quarter at £2.17s.6d. an ounce is £29.10s. and 6d.; there's the coin, sir." Now all this shaking and rousing is to make the gold dust pass through the top sheet, and when he reverses the sheets and the punctures are no longer on top the green and victimized miner may examine them without suspicion.

Duncan MacDonald

I know no place in the world, however, where more wit is required or, better, where a larger amount of small cunning is the *sine qua non* for getting on in life than Cariboo. If your seller should be a Yankee, it will run hard with him if he does not have the best of the bargain. The Yankee axiom in the sales at Cariboo is that, the higher the sum wanted for the gold claim, the greater the proof of its value. I have known Cariboo claims offered, ay and sold too, for as much as 100,000 dollars when they were not worth five dollars, or would not pay the cost of developing. On the other hand, I once had a claim there myself for which I asked 3,000 dollars, a fair price in the English sense of the term, but the claim was summarily condemned because of my low valuation of it; whereas if I had been unprincipled enough to put it up at 20,000, it would have assuredly found a ready purchaser.

Francis Poole

The Mucho Oro Claim, Stout's Gulch, Cariboo, B.C., c.1867-70. Photo by: Frederick Dally

115

N. 80. Cristine McDonald. Daughter of
H. B. C. chief trader at Fort Colville.

1860-61. Photo by: Royal Engineers

Sometimes to English and even to Canadian ears it sounds well when a settler reports his marriage to the daughter of an Indian chief. A young Englishman, well connected at home, who has been for some years a resident in the wilds of British Columbia, wrote to his friends that he had formed such an alliance. His mother, thinking that his marriage was somewhat similar to that of Smith with the daughter of Pocahontas, and regarding her daughter-in-law as a native princess, sent out to her a beautiful satin dress as a wedding present. The poor squaw could hardly understand its use and had no conception of its value. A pair of blankets would really have been a more appropriate gift.

Rev. Daniel Gordon

116

Spokane Garry

In this same hell of the wilderness I found Spokane Garry, one of the lads already mentioned as having been sent to Red River for their education.... On his return to his countrymen he had, for a time, endeavoured to teach them to read and write; but he had gradually abandoned the attempt, assigning as his reason or his pretext that the others "jawed him so much about it." He forthwith relapsed into his original barbarism, taking to himself as many wives as he could get; and then, becoming a gambler, he lost both all that he had of his own and all that he could beg or borrow from others. He was evidently ashamed of his proceedings, for he would not come out of the tent to shake hands even with an old friend.

George Simpson

"Garry, a Spokane Chief", Fort Colville, Washington, 1860-61.
Photo by: Royal Engineers

117

Snags

Snags, which form the most dangerous impediment to the navigation of rivers like the Fraser, are large trees which, having been carried down the stream to a shallow spot, become firmly embedded there. As a rule they float down the river heavy end first so that when they stick the upper part of the trunk opposes the stream and is worn by it to a sharp point, in many cases sufficiently below the surface to be hidden from the steersman's eye.

Going up against the current, therefore, at a comparatively slow pace, the steamer can afford to disregard the snags; for if she strikes on one, it is easy to shut off the steam and drift back from it. But spinning down the current, it is a very serious matter for one of these large unwieldy boats to become transfixed upon a well-rooted, obstinate snag. In some spots of the Fraser an awkward snag may equally impede the navigation of a steamer up or down the stream. One, known as the Umatilla Snag, from a steamer of that name having first struck upon it, lies in a very narrow and rapid bend of the river at which, from the swiftness of the current, the steamer is very liable to be caught and drifted back upon it after, as she imagined, having safely passed it. Upon one occasion, when I was going up the river in the *Enterprise*, no less than three times after we had struggled past the snag the strong current caught and swung us broadside across the stream; and it was only by running the vessel's bow into the muddy bank without a moment's hesitation and holding her there by the nose, as it were, until she recovered breath to make another effort, that we escaped impalement. There was something very exciting in this struggle between the forces of steam and water. Each time as we hung by the bank the engineer might be heard below freshening his fires and getting up as much steam as the boilers could, or might not, bear for the next effort. The wheel-house in these vessels is situated forward, so that there is almost direct communication between it and the engine room. By the helm stands the captain. "Ho! Frank," he hails down the tube, "how much steam have you?" "So many pounds," is Frank's reply. "Guess you must give her ten pounds more, or we shan't get past that infernal snag." And then more stoking is heard below, and the unpleasant feeling comes over the listener that the boilers lie just beneath his feet and that, if anything should happen to them, there can be no doubt about his fate. But presently Frank's voice sounds again. "All ready, Cap'n: can't give her any more!" The skipper loses no time; "Stand by, then!" is his response. Then, to the men forward, who have made a rope fast to some stump on the bank to keep the boat from dropping off, "Let go!" and she falls off for a second or two; her bow cants out a little: "Ting! ting! ting!" goes the engine-room bell, the signal for full speed ahead; every timber of the lightly built vessel trembles. We watch the trees on the bank eagerly to see if she moves ahead. Presently she drops a little but her head is still kept up; then the stream catches her on one bow and, if the bottom should be hard and rocky or the water deeper than was thought, away she flies down the river until she is brought up against the bank or across the snag.

The perseverance of the Yankee skipper in overcoming these difficulties is certainly remarkable. Upon one occasion, after making four unsuccessful efforts to steam past this Umatilla Snag, all the men had to be landed and track her past the dangerous spot. Further up it was found necessary to resort to the same tedious process, and the united strength of crew and passengers with difficulty got her over a few hundred yards in the space of two hours, "Frank" below in his engine room cramming on all the steam he could to help us. Nor is the composure with which the captain meets and remedies an accident less remarkable. A supply of tarred blankets is always kept handy for service and, if a hole is stove in the steamer's bottom, the captain coolly runs her ashore on the nearest convenient shoal, jams as many blankets into the crevice as seem necessary, nails down a few boards over them, and continues his journey composedly. He is often reduced to very serious straits, no doubt, and is not at all particular in the use of means to master a difficulty. I was assured by a passenger on the *Enterprise* to Hope in 1859 that he saw the contents of a cask of bacon turned on to the fires when additional steam to pass a troublesome rapid was necessary.

R.C. Mayne

Building the Victoria at the mouth of the Quesnel River, B.C., c.1867-70. Photo by: Frederick Dally

Hazelton

Several bands of Indians live and hunt in the vicinity of the Forks. They are generally of a peaceable disposition and work for the whites with alacrity and goodwill. About three miles from Hazelton...the Indians have thrown a suspension bridge across the rocky chasm through which the waters of the Wotsonqua rush with impetuous haste towards the Skeena. Here the scenery is wild and sufficiently picturesque to please the most ardent lover of nature. The bridge is built entirely of wood fastened together by withes and branches; its height above the roaring waters beneath is fifty feet, and it sways about under the weight of a man to try even the nerves of a Blondin....

Tom Hankin and I, accompanied by Charlie and another Indian, started on a little tour up the Wotsonqua, taking with us my camera which Tom, facetiously and, as it turned out, unfortunately, chose to designate by the rather inappropriate name of the "Cholera Box." In order to explain, it is necessary to remark that a few months previous Mr. T., the gentleman in charge of the mission station at the mouth of the Naas River, had paid a pastoral visit to the Achwylget Indians. With his other impedimenta he had brought a small magic lantern and slides, which were duly exhibited to their wondering gaze, not without a certain amount of pomp and ceremony. After the reverend gentleman's's departure, however, it most unfortunately happened that a species of cholera broke out among the natives, the origin of which they most illogically attributed to the "one-eyed devil" in the lantern and its exhibitor. Once possessed of the idea, which the native medicine men did their utmost to encourage, the reasoning and arguments of the whites were unavailing; and as the disease spread, so did the belief in the occult powers of Mr. T —— gain ground.... With this unfortunate precedent the reader may imagine that I was not unnaturally a little shy of parading the camera, an instrument bearing a certain family likeness to the hated lantern, and which my friend Tom would persist in calling by such an obnoxious name. As luck would have it, after we were out a couple of days, the Indian who made the photographic apparatus his particular burden was taken suddenly ill one evening in camp. We had noticed certain peculiarities in his behaviour and had, on several occasions, observed him eyeing the dreaded box with looks of evident aversion. When turning in on that particular evening, Tom remarked in his sententious way: "I'll bet the treats that fellow's berth will be vacant tomorrow morning." And when we got up the following day we found his prophetic speech verified, for no Indian was to be seen but Charlie, who said the fellow had gone off, evidently in mortal terror of the box and its mysterious contents. Tom and I thus fell in for equal shares of the remaining load while Charlie, being a Haida and above such superstitious fears, shouldered the box without comment....

Upon several occasions during this little tour we came upon the remains of the Western Union Telegraph Company's line, and at one particular stage of our trip followed for several miles the wide and well cut-out trail which had been opened for that purpose. The reader may possibly not be aware of the fact that, several years ago, the Western Union constructed a telegraph line from Quesnel to Fort Stager, intending to carry it northwards to Bering's straits where by a cable it was to have connected with the Asiatic shores and, after being carried over the vast Siberian steppes, with Europe. This was previous to the successful termination of the North Atlantic Company's operations which, of course, put a stop to further attempts in this direction. The wide and thoroughly cut-out trail still remains, but the poles have been ruthlessly cut down by the Indians, who stole the insulators and made use of the wire for various purposes. Tons of that expensive material still lie in the dreary depths of the British Columbian forests, while immense coils are yet in store at the now deserted post, Fort Stager, the relics of a vast undertaking and a silent tribute to American enterprise.

Charles Horetzky

Indian suspension bridge over the Wotsonqua River, B.C., 1872. Photo by: Charles Horetzky

Junction of the North and South Thompson Rivers at Kamloops, B.C., 1871. Photo by: Benjamin Baltzly

122

Salmon caches, Yale, B.C., c.1870. Photo by: Frederick Dally

I entered into a discussion with Quaw as to the benefit to be derived from a cheap sale of salmon. Among other things I told him he would certainly have a fair chance of going to heaven when he died, all of which being spoken in the chaste language of the Chinook he took into his heart. The end of it was that after breakfast he handed over 650 salmon at ten cents each, and he also helped to pack them on the two dog-sleds. The noble red man is a strange individual. Last summer when the salmon were running up the river and we wanted some fresh, Quaw wanted us to pay $1.50 each for them; now after having cured and dried them he sells ten for one dollar.

Charles Hanington

123

Canyon Road

Five days' driving brought us to the terrific road between Lytton and Yale, and as we sat in the wagon within a few inches of the unguarded edge of the precipice of 700 or 800 feet, running up and down the steeps, and along the narrow portions, winding round the face of the bluffs, we could not help an uneasy consciousness that a very trifling accident might eject us from our lofty position into the depths below. And what made matters look worse was that our carriage was gradually coming to pieces. First one spring broke, and then another, and we bumped about on the axles. Next the splinter-bar gave way and had to be tied up with a piece of rope. All these would have been trifling accidents had the road been of a different character but when, to crown all, the pole snapped in its socket and the wagon ran into the horses, we had good cause to be thankful that this had happened in the middle of a flat, just after crossing the suspension bridge. Had it occurred a few minutes sooner we should doubtless have been precipitated headlong into the roaring canyons. The pole was past mending, so the driver took the horses out and led them back to a house about half a mile distant, the rest of us remaining behind to guard the treasure by the light of a large bonfire, for it was already quite dark. In about an hour the driver reappeared, accompanied by a friend, bringing a large covered wagon drawn by two fine Californian horses. The fresh horses were put in as leaders and we soon started with our four-in-hand, rattling along at a headlong gallop, for we had now two drivers, one who managed the reins while the other vigorously plied the whip. The express-man had brought a bottle of whisky back with him, and he and his friend devoted themselves assiduously to it in the calmer intervals of their joint occupation. After a time it was discovered that the reins of the leaders were not crossed, and consequently useless for guiding purposes; but the two Californians led the way admirably, sweeping round every curve with great precision. Much of the road was as dangerous as any we had passed before but the men shouted and whipped up, the horses galloped furiously, the wagon whisked round the precipitous bluffs and tore down the steep descents in mad career. We reached Yale before midnight, having been little more than an hour doing the last fifteen miles of this fearful road.

Milton and Cheadle

Breakdown

Mr. Hamilton's foot was pressing firmly against the lever of the brake as the coach rolled swiftly down a long incline, one of the last ere the level river valley was finally reached. All at once the iron bar broke from the driver's foot, the heavy vehicle, released from control, drove forward upon the wheelers, and Mr. Hamilton with difficulty retained his seat in the shock of the unlooked-for catastrophe. But he was equal to the emergency. He pulled himself and his team together in an instant; then he whipped his leaders and held on down the long incline; the pace grew faster and faster, the inside passengers, knowing nothing of the accident, and deeming that the usual "trot for the avenue" had been changed into a wild gallop to that destination, cheered lustily.

At the foot of the hill the coach was pulled up. Mr. Hamilton, descending, surveyed the brake. "Clean gone," he said, remounting. "Guess we'd 'ave bin clean gone too, if it 'ad happened back at Chinaman's Bluff or Jackass Mountain." Then he drove into Yale.

William Francis Butler

Cariboo Road in the Fraser Canyon at Seventeen Mile Bluff, B.C., c.1868. Photo by: Frederick Dally

Columbia Street, New Westminster, B.C., c.1869. Photo by: Frederick Dally

Indian encampment on the Fraser River, B.C., 1867-68. Photo by: Frederick Dally

Man

Of all the strange sights in the wilderness there is nothing so strange as man — strange not only to the wild things, but to man himself. Nor is it difficult to comprehend why it should be so. If a bear were to escape from a menagerie and perambulate a crowded street, he would doubtless be vastly astonished at the cabs, and the men, and the omnibuses; but it is by no means improbable that he would be still more vastly astonished if he were to meet another bear perambulating there too. So is it when we reverse the cases. When one has lived long in the solitude, a moose or a buffalo gladdens the eye; but if one wants excitement it is fully experienced when the vision of the human animal strikes the wanderer's sight.

William Francis Butler

Atrocity

After getting through the core of the Cascade range he came upon the "Murderers' camp," where thirteen of Waddington's men were murdered eight years ago. The spot looks as if it had never before been visited by man since the massacre. The number of tents could be counted by the cedar bark forming the beds. Strewed around were various tools — a blacksmith's anvil, sledge hammers, crowbars, grindstone, vice, picks, and half a dozen shovels carefully placed against a tree ready for the morrow's work; also pieces of clothing, amongst which were at least one pair of woman's boots — too surely indicating the source of the trouble. This last clause suggests the origin of more than one "Indian atrocity." It's a fair question to ask always, "Who struck the first blow?"

George Grant

Jungle

On the 31st of July we left in a pouring rain and plunged into the pathless forest before us. We were at once brought up by the steep face of a hill which came down close to the water's edge. But the steepness of the path was not the greatest difficulty. No one who has not seen a primeval forest, where trees of gigantic size have grown and fallen undisturbed for ages, can form any idea of the collection of timber or the impenetrable character of such a region. There were pines and thujas of every size, the patriarch of 300 feet in height standing alone or thickly clustering groups of young ones struggling for the vacant place of some prostrate giant. The fallen trees lay piled around, forming barriers often six or eight feet high on every side: trunks of huge cedars, moss-grown and decayed, lay half-buried in the ground on which others as mighty had recently fallen; trees still green and living, recently blown down, blocking the view with the walls of earth held in their matted roots; living trunks, dead trunks, rotten trunks; dry, barkless trunks and trunks moist and green with moss; bare trunks and trunks with branches — prostrate, reclining, horizontal, propped up at different angles; timber of every size, in every stage of growth and decay, in every possible position, entangled in every possible combination. The swampy ground was densely covered with American dogwood and elsewhere with thickets of the aralea, a tough-stemmed trailer, with leaves as large as those of the rhubarb plant and growing in many places as high as our shoulders. Both stem and leaves are covered with sharp spines which pierced our clothes as we forced our way through the tangled growth, and made the legs and hands of the pioneers scarlet from the inflammation of myriads of punctures.

Milton and Cheadle

Indian home at Burrard Inlet (Vancouver), B.C., c.1867-70. Photo by: Frederick Dally

Scene on the Tranquille River near Kamloops, B.C., 1871. Photo by: Benjamin Baltzly

You must imagine our camp then tonight. Opposite sit the Indians, Johnny as usual silent and impassive, the other two with their heads in their hands sobbing out their grief as usual too. On my right is my worthy chief Jarvis, very thin, very white, and very much subdued. He is thinking of a good many things, I suppose, like the rest of us. On my left is Alex chewing tobacco and looking about used up.... I do believe that we have not many more days to live. I have been thinking of "the dearest spot on earth to me," of our mother and father, of all my brothers and sisters and friends. Of the happy days at home, of all the good deeds I have left undone and all the bad ones committed. I wonder if ever our bones will be discovered, when and by whom, if our friends will mourn long for us, or do as is often done, forget us as soon as possible.

Charles Hanington

PART IV

THE WEST COAST

Immigration

The only route practicable for poor families till a wagon road can be constructed from Red River to British Columbia across British territory is that via Cape Horn. This involves a voyage of between four and five months — not a much longer period, however, than is spent in going to New Zealand.... The vessels that are acknowledged to combine in the highest degree comfort, safety, and expedition are those belonging to the Hudson's Bay Company. One sails from London in spring and another in autumn, making the passage in about four months....

I would urge upon individuals and families resolved to proceed by the Horn *route* the importance of using strict caution and making careful enquiry in selecting a ship, though her owners should possess high commercial reputation and her qualities be grandly paraded in advertisements. If the vessel be old, there is danger; if her staterooms be dingy, the effect upon the spirits of crew and passengers will be obvious. Let personal inspection be made also of the stores, as far as possible. The character and bearing of the captain should be well ascertained; a good ship may be rendered utterly intolerable under the direction of a bad commander....

A vessel should be chosen that has a height of not less than six or seven feet between decks, and compartments roomy. If the condition of your exchequer necessitates that you should go in the steerage, get near the centre of the vessel, where motion is least felt. Procure if you can a berth extending *lengthwise* in the ship, else the inconvenience of having your feet raised occasionally higher than your head will have to be sustained. If a wife and family be in the party, it should be seen that not only the berths are sufficiently wide but that ample space is reserved for keeping private stores and such other comforts as forethought may deem to be needful for the voyage. Steerage passengers, who may arrange with the owners to furnish their own provisions, should be very particular as to where they buy. Instances could be related of heartless imposition practised by dealers in ship's stores upon unsuspecting emigrants. The most agreeable and economical method of emigrating is for a company having business, tastes, religious denomination, or some other common tie to unite in preparation for the voyage and place themselves under voluntary discipline in relation to each other. Information in regard to suitable outfits for the voyage may be obtained by consulting friends who have gone through the experience of a four or five months' passage, or from any respectable outfitter in Liverpool or London. The outfit of a miner having come to the country and about to proceed to Victoria for the mines of British Columbia or Vancouver Island usually consists of the following articles: two woollen shirts, four pairs of worsted socks, a pair of leather top-boots, a pair of Indian-rubber mining-boots, a strong pair of trousers, an Indian-rubber coat, two pairs of blankets, a small tent.

No British colonies encounter such gigantic hindrances to progress and settlement as those to which the attention of the reader is directed. They contain every element adapted to contribute to the happiness and wealth of every class of emigrants. But being situated on the extreme western verge of British North America, they are the most remote and inconvenient of approach of all our dependencies. It takes what many an industrious artisan would esteem a fortune to transfer a large family to them from England by the Panama route. Several months and no inconsiderable amount of money is expended, in adopting the cheapest and yet most tedious route via Cape Horn.

Matthew Macfie

Crew of H.M.S. Mutine, c.1869. Photo by: Frederick Dally

Part of the British Pacific Fleet in Esquimalt Harbour, B.C., 1867-70. Photo by: Frederick Dally

Esquimalt, Vancouver Island, B.C., 1867-68. Photo by: Frederick Dally

A certain description of immigrants fresh from England imagine in their verdant simplicity that their recent arrival from that great centre of knowledge and civilization gives them a right to patronize colonists whose condition they deem benighted from long exile. The class I refer to have a weakness for manufacturing stories of better days, departed greatness, and rich relations. One person whom I knew professed to be a University man; to have been familiar with a European prince; heir of a large estate and ward of a gentleman of influence in England. The curiosity of a friend being excited to learn particulars respecting the mysterious history he supposed to attach to this hero, wrote home to parties claimed by him as former associates. On investigation it appeared that he was a bankrupt draper and an outlaw who had changed his name.

One lady, who had contracted the inconvenient habit of dropping her h's and using singular verbs with plural nouns, provoked enquiry into the past by expatiating on the magnificence of her ancestral mansion — the number of storeys it contained, its turrets and battlements, and the fine view of the sea it commanded. The fact was, to speak without figure, she was the daughter of a worthy lighthouse-keeper.

Matthew Macfie

135

Canoes

I had hardly completed my investigation of the canoe, its crew, and contents when, to my intense astonishment, the four Indians lifted me as they would a bale of fur or a barrel of pork and without a word deposited me in the bottom of the canoe, where I was enjoined to sit, much in the same position enforced on a culprit in the parish stocks. I may mention, incidentally, that a canoe is not half as enjoyable as poets and novelists, who are prone to draw imaginary sketches, would lead the uninitiated to believe. It would be impossible to trust oneself in a more uncomfortable, dangerous, damp, disagreeable kind of boat — generally designated a "fairy barque", that "rides, dances, glides, threads its silvery course over seas and lakes or, arrow-like, shoots foaming rapids." All a miserable delusion and a myth! Getting in (unless lifted, as I was, bodily, like baggage) is to any but an Indian a dangerous and difficult process; the least preponderance of weight to either side and out you tumble into the water to a certainty. Again, lowering oneself into the bottom is quite as bad, if not worse, requiring extreme care to keep an even balance and a flexibility of back and limb seldom possessed by any save tumblers and tightrope dancers. Down safely, then, as I have said, you are compelled to sit in a most painful position, and the least attempt to alter it generally results in a sudden heeling-over of the canoe and you find yourself sitting in a foot of cold water.

John Keast Lord

Shells

Some years ago the frigate *Sutlej* shelled one of the villages, the Ahowsett, for an outrage on a small trading craft. Of course the Indians all cleared out into the bush and the casualties were small. Subsisting, however, as they do, almost entirely on fish, the destruction of their canoes is a fearful punishment. It would be easy to exterminate them all in that way. The *Sutlej*'s shell, however, did some damage in the long run, as several unexploded ones having been found in the forest in the rear of the village, some of the ingenious Indians proceeded to extract the fuses with cold chisels to get at the powder, the natural result being that some half a dozen of them came to grief.

Charles Horetzky

Thrift

I must not omit to mention that most of the Indians are good shots at a fixed object, but they never think of firing at a bird on the wing. Nothing excites their admiration more than to see birds shot flying, but I could never get them to try it. No doubt a great reason for this is their scanty supply of powder and shot; they are always begging for these, and will barter almost anything for them. Their mode of approaching wild fowl is very curious and characteristic: a man will take a small canoe and fill the bows with branches of evergreens so as completely to conceal himself seated behind it. Through the middle of this hedge he points his gun, letting the barrel rest along the stem of the canoe. He then paddles the canoe very quietly along in the direction of a number of birds sitting on the water, taking care to keep the bows straight towards them: the birds are very sharp, and will swim across the canoe to ascertain if there is any deception; but as they all go one way the man is able to keep the canoe facing them, and they fancy it is a floating bush. So careful are these men of their powder, however, that they are not generally content to get within shot of one bird, but will manoeuvre about till they can get two or three in a line. I have seen them devote half a day to this, perhaps only firing once in several hours.

R.C. Mayne

Chinook-style canoes, Vancouver Island, B.C., 1867-70. Photo by: Frederick Dally

Victoria

We were landed soon after our arrival on a rocky point of land with a snug sheltered bay on each side; an easy slope led up to the frame of a house, destined to be our headquarters; a pretty spot, very English-like in its general features, but in the rough clothing of uncultivated nature. Tents were pitched, the baggage carried safely up and stowed away, and the first camp of the Boundary Commission established in this new land of promise.

Our first walk to Victoria, now the thriving capital of Vancouver Island, was made on the evening of our landing. The gold fever was just beginning to rage fast and furiously, and all classes from every country were pouring in — a very torrent of gold hunters. Not that gold hunter means only he that digs and washes the yellow ore from out Nature's treasury, but includes a herd of parasites that sap the gains of the honest digger, tempting him to gamble, drink poison (miscalled whisky), and purchase trashy trumpery made only to sell, and thus fool away his wealth, "earned like a horse, squandered like an ass!" Both species were well represented in what could not, in any sense of the word, as yet be called a town.

The old trading post of the Hudson's Bay Company, the governor's house, and a few scattered residences of the chief traders and other employees of the Company alone represented the permanent dwellings. But in all directions were canvas tents, from the white strip stretched over a ridge-pole and pegged to the ground (affording just room enough for two to crawl in and sleep) to the great canvas store, a blaze of light, redolent of cigars, cobblers, and cocktails. The rattle of the dice box, the droning invitation of the keepers of the monte tables, the discordant sounds of badly-played instruments, angry words, oaths too terrible to name, roistering songs with noisy refrains, were all signs significant of the golden talisman that met me on every side as I elbowed my way amidst the unkempt throng that were awaiting means of conveyance to take them to the auriferous bars of the far-famed Fraser River. Along the side of the harbour, wherever advantageous water sites were obtainable, the noise of busy industry sounded pleasantly in contrast to the mingled hubbub I had just left. Higher up the slope substantial stores were being rapidly built. Out of these germs grew the present town, the capital of the island.

John Keast Lord

Fortune Hunters

The chief misfortune connected with the influx of population at this period was that it comprised an excessive proportion of clerks, retired army officers, prodigal sons, and a host of other romantic nondescripts who indulged visions of sudden wealth obtainable with scarcely more exertion than is usually put forth in a pleasure excursion to the continent of Europe. These trim young fellows exhibited a profusion of leather coats and leggings, assuming a sort of defiant air, the interpretation of which was, "We are the men to show you 'Colonials' how to brave danger and fatigue!" But their pretensions generally evaporated with the breath by which they were expressed, and many that set out with this dare-all aspect were soon thankful to be permitted to break stones, chop wood, serve as stable boys, or root out tree stumps. The vague imaginations with which they left home were soon dissipated when, on the termination of the voyage, they discovered that 500 miles lay between them and Cariboo — a distance which must be passed over muddy roads and frowning precipices with whatever necessaries might be required for the trip strapped to their shoulders. Hundreds went halfway to the mines and returned in despondency; hundreds more remained in Victoria, and were only saved from starvation by the liberality of more prosperous citizens. A much larger number came than the country, with a deficient supply of roads, was prepared to receive. Still a considerable number made large amounts of money, and the majority of those who have possessed sufficient fortitude to bear inconveniences and battle against discouragements are in a fair way for speedily acquiring a competency.

Matthew Macfie

"How we passed our time on board the Oregon steamer":
Lieut.-Gov. Frederick Seymour and friends at New Westminster,
B.C., 1864. Photo by: Charles Gentile

"As we appeared on arrival in B.C.": Lieut.-Gov. Frederick
Seymour and friends at his residence in New Westminster, B.C.,
1864. Photo by: Charles Gentile

Nanaimo, Vancouver Island, B.C., c.1870 (photographer's portable developing box in foreground). Photo by: Richard Maynard

Scandal

I have witnessed scenes after sunset calculated to shock even the bluntest sensibilities. The fires of Indian tents pitched upon the beach casting a lurid glare upon the water; the loud and discordant whoopings of the natives, several of whom were usually infuriated with bad liquor; the crowds of the more debased miners strewed in vicious concert with squaws on the public highway presented a spectacle diabolical in the extreme. Even now one cannot walk from the ferry up the Esquimalt road by day or by night without encountering the sight of these Indian slaves squatting in considerable numbers in the bush, for what purpose it is not difficult to imagine, and the extent to which the nefarious practices referred to are encouraged by the crews of Her Majesty's ships is a disgrace to the service they represent and a scandal to the country. Hundreds of dissipated white men, moreover, live in open concubinage with these wretched creatures. So unblushingly is this traffic carried on that I have seen the husband and wife of a native family canvassing from one miner's shanty to another with the view of making assignations for the squaws in their possession. On one occasion I saw an Indian woman offering to dispose of her own child — the offspring of a guilty alliance with a white man — for £3, at the door of a respectable white dwelling.

Matthew Macfie

Cowichan Indians, Vancouver Island, B.C., 1867-70.
Photo by: Frederick Dally

Umbrella

I managed to escape through the pickets at the back of the fort and, stealthily reaching the beach under cover of the trees, imagined myself safe. A light misty rain fell thickly, and a flock of sanderlings, running along in the ripple, completely absorbed my attention. I was suddenly startled by hearing the "crunch, crunch" of a foot in the shingle behind me. I had looked right and left on reaching the beach, but not a trace of Indian was visible. Turning suddenly round you can picture my surprise at finding myself face to face with a savage, unclad from head to heel, carrying — what should you imagine? — not a scalping knife, or a war club, or bow or spear or gory scalp: it was an immense green gingham umbrella with horn crook, battered brass ferule, furled with a ring such as curtains are hung on. He politely offered me a part and, scarcely deeming it safe to refuse, I paraded the beach linked arm-in-arm with the ugliest specimen of humanity eyes ever beheld. I wonder if, before or since, a naked savage and civilized man ever walked together on the sea-beach, listening to "what the wild waves were saying", sheltered from the rain by a green gingham umbrella! I trow not. I should have been no more astonished at seeing a seal, or old Neptune himself, with an umbrella than I was at a naked Indian so protected on the beach at Fort Rupert.

John Keast Lord

141

Fort Street, looking east, Victoria, B.C., 1867-70. Photo by: Frederick Dally

Chinese

All the domestic servants we had seen as yet were Chinamen. They are paid from $20 to $45 a month but, as servant girls ask nearly as much, "John" is usually preferred. Though all gamble and most smoke opium, such vices do not materially interfere with their duties as servants. They are bowling out not only the cooks and servant girls but the washer-women on the Pacific coast. And we must look to them as the future navvies and miners of our West. There are now 18,000 of them in San Francisco out of a population of 160,000; 60,000 in California, and about 100,000 altogether on the Pacific side of North America.... Is it wonderful, then, that there should be a prejudice against them in the breasts of the white working-classes they are supplanting? The true-blue Briton of last century hated the French because "they were all slaves and wore wooden shoes." Why should not the labourer hate the Chinese, when they not only wear wooden shoes but are the best of workmen, cleanly, orderly, patient, industrious, and above all cheap?

George Grant

It is natural that a race so exclusive and so much avoided by their white fellow-citizens on the coast should give preference to the manufactures of their own country. Much of the clothing they wear and many of their articles of food came from China.... But it is a mistake to regard the trade done and the capital acquired by them as so much wealth diverted from the channels of white industry, since but for their presence in the country the greater part of that trade would not have been created; nor would that capital have been accumulated. They cannot prevent commercial advantage accruing to the colonies from their influence, if they would. It is often British bottoms that convey them from China, and they are obliged to buy hardware, waterproof boots, and pork from us. Poultry, too, being esteemed a great luxury, is in great demand among them. When they have lived among the civilized for a time, it not unfrequently happens that they adopt the European and American costume attire.

Matthew Macfie

Chinese servants at Government House, Victoria, B.C., 1867-70. Photo by: Frederick Dally

Law and Order

The only occasions on which the extreme penalty of the law has been put in force since the advent of the whites in Vancouver Island have been in connection with Indian atrocities. In one case, a Songhish native was executed for the murder of a sailor belonging to one of Her Majesty's ships. This man, on his way from Victoria to Esquimalt in a state of inebriation, one evening entered the dwelling of his destroyer and attempted to take liberties with the squaw of the Siwash. The latter, stung by the insult, stabbed the sailor. Doubtless the verdict of the jury and the sentence of the Court were according to the evidence, but the provocation ought to have been accepted as in some degree palliative of the bloody deed. It is questionable whether, had the crime been committed by one white man against another under like circumstances, the claims of justice would have been exacted with so much rigour. Nine-tenths of the outrages perpetrated by natives upon the superior race and supposed to be the result of insensate cruelty can be traced to some wanton violation of the personal or domestic rights of the Indians on the part of the whites.... The principal and immediate effect of contact between the representatives of civilization and the aborigines has been that "firewater", debauchery, syphilitic disease, and augmented mortality have been introduced. Appalling as the anomaly may appear, it is nevertheless uniform that the nation which professes to bring into a virgin colony the blessings of the gospel in one hand, carries a moral Pandora box in the other, accomplishing the physical and moral ruin of the primitive inhabitants whose interests, gratitude, and respect should prompt it jealously to guard.

Matthew Macfie

The Party

March 15th — We gave a ball to the fair ladies here; two of the men-of-war, the *Satellite* and *Plumper*, with ourselves determined to join together and give a grand ball to the ladies of Vancouver Island. I was appointed one of the ball committee with some others and we set our heads together to do the best we could in this part of the world. The first thing was to find a place large enough for the occasion and the only house we could find was the market-place, a most dismal-looking place, enough to drive all thoughts of dancing out of one's head. However, we got all the flags we could from the ships and turned in thirty or forty sailors, and in a short time a fairy palace of flags was erected so that not a particle of the building was visible; we then rigged up some large chandeliers and sconces of bayonets and ramrods wreathed with evergreens which, when lighted up, produced a regular blaze of light and made it quite a fairy scene. We also got up a large supper room in the same style and managed to provide a first-rate supper. Everybody came to the ball from the Governor downwards, nearly 200 in all, and we kept the dancing up with great spirit till half past three in the morning. Everybody was quite delighted with it and it goes by the name of "the Party" par excellence; nobody says "ball" in this part of the world, it is always party. The ladies were nicely dressed and some of them danced very well, though they would look much better if they would only learn to wear their crinoline properly. It is most lamentable to see the objects they make of themselves, some of the hoops being quite oval, whilst others had only one hoop rather high up, the remainder of the dress hanging down perpendicularly.... After the ball we had to escort most of the young ladies home, for you must know that there are very few vehicles in this country and most of the progression is on foot. I conveyed some ladies home who lived about a mile out of the town. You would have laughed to have seen us at that time of night floundering away through the mud, the ladies with their ball dresses tied up round their waists and long boots on, your distant brother smoking a very long cigar and "standing by", as the sailors say, to help any unfortunate petticoat who should become irretrievably stuck in the mud; however, young ladies here are not so dreadfully afraid of wet feet as some in England and everybody got home in safety without feeling any ill effects. I finally turned into bed at half past six on the morning of March 16th. At twelve o'clock most of us met at a large breakfast, after which my health was drunk in some very indifferent champagne and we all separated to our respective abodes.

Charles Wilson

"The Birdcages", central portion of Government Buildings, Victoria, B.C., 1867-70. Photo by: Frederick Dally

Members of the first Parliament of British Columbia, 1864. Photo by: Charles Gentile

The immigrant accustomed to the distinctions of class obtaining in settled populations of the old world will be struck to observe how completely the social pyramid is inverted in the colonies. Many persons of birth and education but of reduced means are compelled for a time after their arrival to struggle with hardship, while the vulgar, who have but recently acquired wealth, are arrayed in soft clothing and fare sumptuously. Sons of admirals and daughters of clergymen are sometimes found in abject circumstances, while men only versed in the art of wielding the butcher's knife, the drayman's whip, and the blacksmith's hammer, or women of low degree, have made fortunes. The most ludicrous example of these social transpositions with which I am acquainted relates to a gentleman and his manservant who came out together in the same ship. The hireling, having quarrelled with his master, resigned his situation, applied for employment in the police force, and was accepted. The first subject on whom he found an opportunity of practising officially after he was appointed happened to be his former master. That unfortunate gentleman laid himself open to the suspicion of being "drunk and disorderly", and was immediately taken in charge by the individual who had been wont to serve him.

Matthew Macfie

146

John Muir's lumber mill, Sooke, Vancouver Island, B.C., c.1867-70. Photo by: Frederick Dally

Visiting

The least experienced eye could see the capabilities of the site of Victoria for a town and that it was capable, should the occasion ever arise, of springing into importance as Melbourne or San Francisco had done. As it was, the place was very pleasant and society — as it is generally in a young colony — frank and agreeable. No ceremony was known in those pleasant times. All the half-dozen houses that made up the town were open to us. In fine weather, riding parties of the gentlemen and ladies of the place were formed and we returned generally to a high tea, or tea-dinner, at Mr. Douglas's or Mr. Work's, winding up the pleasant evening with dance and song. We thought nothing then of starting off to Victoria in sea-boots, carrying others in our pockets, just to enjoy a pleasant evening by a good log fire. And we cared as little for the weary tramp homeward to Esquimalt in the dark, although it happened sometimes that men lost their way and had to sleep in the bush all night.

R.C. Mayne

Insanity

The intense pitch to which the feelings of people are strung in a gold-producing country is a frequent cause of insanity. Whether that malady exist in a greater degree in this community than in one of a more settled description I am not sufficiently versed in the statistics of the subject to aver. But certainly a much larger proportion of cases have been personally known to me here than in the same period I ever saw in the much denser populations of England. I can reckon up eight persons — all of whom I have been on speaking terms with and most of whom I knew intimately — who, in four years and a half, have become lunatics and as such are either living or dead.

There was a quiet and respectable man, about thirty, who kept a school in Victoria. He became unmanned by pecuniary difficulties and took leave of friends he had been visiting with unusual seriousness and formality, and the same evening attached a rope to the wall of his room, thence suspending himself by the neck. Two days after, the owner of the apartment went to collect the rent and cut the body down.

Two other unfortunate persons laboured under the hallucination that certain friends had conspired to mix poison with their food. Another was a medical man, who called on me, offering for sale a very old copy of an Italian Bible which he assured me was valued by English "book hunters" at a hundred pounds; but being embarrassed he was willing to let me have it for ten pounds. Still he never produced the book. The occasion of his narrow circumstances was related by him with great earnestness and originality. The local Government, he said, had a spite against him without any provocation, and employed some Chinamen to annoy him by invisible agency. This consisted of a projectile which could be darted through the air at any distance. It was imperceptible to natural vision, but by an affinity established between it and a pimple at the back of the doctor's head, it went straight from the hand which threw it to that object. The result of this contact was that, according to his testimony, he was invariably brought down wherever he might be, unless already in a reclining posture. He went into a learned explanation of the invention of this subtle and dangerous weapon, ascribed by him to the combined genius of a Jesuit priest and a Chinaman, who together brought it to light in the reign of Henry VII. The influence, however, which turned the doctor from a perpendicular to a horizontal position, I fear, answers more correctly to the slang description of Americans: "Chain-lightning, warranted to kill at 100 yards." In plain English, "grog."

Matthew Macfie

View from the St. Nicholas Hotel, Victoria, B.C., 1871. Photo by: Benjamin Baltzly

Indian salmon weir, Cowichan River, Vancouver Island, B.C., 1867-70. Photo by: Frederick Dally

One curious thing at this season of the year is the quantity of dead salmon on the banks of the river; in some of the smaller streams the quantities are so numerous that it produces a most intolerable smell and renders the water anything but pleasant for drinking purposes. Lord, who has been dissecting several of them, thinks this arises from the want of insects to feed the enormous numbers of salmon that run up the rivers. It is a curious thing that you seldom catch a fish here who will give you any play; they generally lie like a dead weight on the line; none of that rush that makes good fishing at home so exciting, indeed I would sooner catch a 3/4 pound trout in an Irish stream than any of the monsters one gets here.

Charles Wilson

150

Modern Science

Sometimes, however, I would allow Chief Klue and his compeers to pay us evening visits. Then, while my men worked and smoked, I spent hours upon hours in explaining the phenomena of nature and arts of civilized man to the chiefs. I found them ever most attentive and interested, and, I must add in justice, far more intelligent than many illiterate white men in our own country. On the other hand, the Indians always believed me to be a great English chieftain — Hyas-King-George-Tyhee (The Queen Charlotte Islands having been discovered in the reign of George the Third, the Indians associate with that king's name every Englishman they have seen since) — by reason of the marvellous tales I used to tell them. The size and population of London and of Europe, the properties of gas and steam, the art of photography, but especially telegraphy, filled them with astonishment. When the chiefs heard how our countrymen could speak together at a distance, and that, ere the present race of Indians were very old, they at Burnaby would be able to converse with their stray friends at Victoria, or with other tribes on the mainland, and without either party moving from their respective positions, they held up their hands amazed. "Powerful is the white man, wise and powerful," exclaimed Klue frequently.

Francis Poole

Haida Chiefs, Skidegate, Queen Charlotte Islands, B.C., 1881.
Photo by: Edward Dossetter

Women at Metlakatla, North-west Coast, B.C., 1881. Photo: Edward Dossetter

I informed him that English ladies were not exchangeable for "goods." He was greatly surprised to hear it, and terribly vexed when, later, I explained our custom in this matter more fully. "Why, then, do your white men come and buy our daughters?" he indignantly exclaimed. And, it must be owned, I was as terribly at a loss how to answer him. The Indian custom is to take a woman to wife for a month on a trial, the usual price asked for a chief's daughter being three blankets. In the event of the damsel not proving a desirable acquisition, she may be sent back within the month. Her relations then return the blankets. It is sad to know that this degrading traffic has been taken advantage of, to an unlimited extent, by the Californian traders who frequent the shores of the North Pacific. I did not wonder, therefore, at Klue's indignation in his discovering the true bearings of their practice.

Francis Poole

Volunteers, Metlakatla, North-west Coast, B.C., 1881. Photo by: Edward Dossetter

Longhouse

The dwellings consist of ten or fifteen rude sheds, about twenty yards long and twelve wide, built of rough cedar planks; the roof a single slant covered with poles and rushes. Six or eight families live in each shed. Every family has its own fire on the ground, and the smoke, that must find its way out as best it can through cracks and holes (chimneys being objected to), hangs in a dense upper cloud so that a man can only keep his head out of it by squatting on the ground: to stand up is to run a risk of suffocation. The children of all ages, in droves, naked and filthy, live under the smoke; as well as squaws, who squat round the smouldering logs; innumerable dogs, like starving wolves, prick-eared, sore-eyed, snappish brutes, unceasingly engaged in faction fights and sudden duels in which the whole pack immediately takes sides. Felt but not heard are legions of bloodthirsty fleas, that would try their best to suck blood from a boot, and by combined exertions would soon flay alive any man with a clean and tender skin.

John Keast Lord

Place of Honour

His house was a largish one, built in the usual Indian way, of wood laid horizontally in light logs and slightly elevated above the ground upon a platform. Despite the sheen of the moon, I looked in vain for the entrance and was beginning to think there must be some Indian dodge in its concealment, with a view probably to providing against sudden attacks, when a young Klootchman lady came tripping along to my assistance. Approaching a big hole three feet in circumference and three feet from the platform's base in the front of the house, she very unceremoniously thrust first one leg through, evidently without touching the bottom on the other side, secondly her head and arms, and finally, by means of a dexterous jerk, dragged the rest of her body after her. This was the door, then, through which the inmates, both male and female, had to scramble whenever they felt disposed to retire to the domestic hearth. The manoeuvres required to accomplish the feat in question were assuredly anything but graceful, especially for a lady: and yet the ladies performed it in the most satisfactory manner, without ever doubling up in a heap on the floor inside. Perforce, I tried the same method myself and, though unsuccessful at the first attempt, I did succeed at the second, greatly to the delight of the pretty Klootchman, who turned out to be Klue's daughter-in-law and my chambermaid for that night.

Other horrors besides the atmosphere now awaited me, for I was assigned the place of honour in the family couch, namely, under the same blanketing with the chief and his daughter, a very interesting young girl, and to lie between them.

Having been paddling away all day as hard as any Indian, I naturally felt anxious to restore my strength with sound, refreshing sleep. Some indefinable sensation, however, seemed to be keeping me awake. I tossed about nearly all night, not much to the comfort of my bedfellows, I should fancy. As the small hours of the morning advanced I found my head inconveniently knocking against an upright pole. Surely a most extraordinary position for a pole, since it undoubtedly served no architectural or ornamental purpose. By degrees this pole gained complete possession of my thoughts and the more I went on thinking, the more persuaded did I become that it had something hideous connected with it. An impulse then seized me to get up and examine it; but as that would have looked like betrayal of fear — a consummation always to be avoided in the presence of savages — I lay still. Presently, an accidental kick from one of the Indians caused the fire to flare. The flare lasted only two or three seconds, yet quite long enough to reveal to my horrified senses at least a hundred scalps fastened round the top of the pole right above me. Fancy my feelings! Despite Klue's professed friendship, and the place of honour I was occupying in the family couch, I instinctively put my hand to my own pole and was not without a throb of thankfulness to find it so far safe. Need it be added that I made my escape as soon as I could prudently do so?

Francis Poole

154

Newitta Village (possibly Bella Coola), North-west Coast, B.C., 1881. Photo by: Edward Dossetter

Head Hunter

I observed a high pole, and dangling from it a head, fresh, bloody, and ghastly; the scalp had been removed, and a rope, passing through the underjaw, served to suspend it. Horribly revolting as the face appeared, still I could not help going close to it. Never had I seen so singular a head; it looked in shape like a sugarloaf, the apex of the skull terminating in a sharp point. On returning to the fort, I inquired if they could tell me anything about this mysterious head. It appeared that, a day or so before our arrival, a war party of the Quakars had returned from a raid on the mainland coast and brought with them a number of slaves. (Prisoners taken in war, or in any other manner, are invariably used as slaves, bought and sold, whipped or killed, as best befits the whim or caprice of their owner.) Amongst the wretched captives was a chief. Soon after landing, he was made fast to a temporary cross erected on the beach, shot, scalped, and beheaded, and it was his head I had seen in my rambles. On hearing further that the tribe to which he belonged was one that elongate instead of flatten the head, I determined at any risk to have the skull. Extreme caution was needed, or a like fate would probably be mine; a white chief's hairless head might possibly adorn the same pole as that of the painted savage. I made several attempts but each time signally failed to accomplish my purpose.

The night proceding our departure, all hopes of obtaining the coveted head were nearly abandoned. Fortune at last smiled upon me; unobserved, I upset the pole, and bagged the head; and pushing it into my game-bag, got safely into the fort. Still in terror of being seen, I hid it in the bastion, and eventually headed it into a pork barrel, with stones and sand; then had it rolled boldly out, and put on board the steamer. On our departure the following morning, I was rejoiced to find the head had not been missed, but somewhat frightened on learning I was to be paddled to the steamer in the state canoe of the chief to whom the trophy belonged. In grand procession we marched from the fort to the canoe, marshalled by the dingy dignitary who, in happy ignorance of the wrong I had done him, was all smiles and grins; the final hand-shaking being accomplished, I was lifted into the canoe in the same fashion as I had been previously lifted out, and rapidly reached the steamer.

The chief came on board the steamer whilst the anchor was being weighed. Imagine what I felt when he seated himself deliberately upon the cask wherein I had hid his property. The wished-for moment came, the wheels splashed slowly round, my plundered friend was bowed over the side, and not until the smoke of the lodge-fires and the fading outline of the village grew dim in the distance did I feel my scalp safe.

John Keast Lord

Patriotism

September 19th — Took the obstreperous chiefs before the commanding officer of the Hecate, who gave them clearly to understand through an interpreter that if they annoyed us again in any way whatsoever he would at once return and burn them out of home and hearth, and that thay must deliver up all the articles they had stolen from us. This action on the part of the Governor will do an incalculable amount of good. It makes us feel a deeper pride in our country and revives the patriotism which too long absence from home is apt to enfeeble.

Francis Poole

Yan, Queen Charlotte Islands, B.C., 1881. Photo by: Edward Dossetter

157

Children

Several instances have occurred of whites being murdered by Indians in different parts of the colony, but I fear these murders have generally been the result of introducing firewater, or taking liberties with the females of the tribe; for although the Indian thinks little of selling female slaves for the vilest purposes, he sometimes avenges an insult offered to his own wives summarily. Their ideas, however, on this subject are by no means clear, for they occasionally take terrible vengeance for an insult which at another time they will not even notice. Whenever a white man takes up his residence among them, they will always supply him with a wife; and if he quits the place and leaves her there, she is not the least disgraced in the eyes of her tribe. The result of this is that you frequently see children quite white, and looking in every respect like English children, at an Indian village, and a very distressing sight it is.

R.C. Mayne

School

I inspect my pupils daily. Some few have ventured to come with their faces painted, but we have less of it daily. A good many too have cast away their nose-rings, yet some come who have very large ones in use still. After schoolteaching was over this morning, a chief remained behind — he had a serious difficulty. His people, who had before decided to give up their medicine-working, were beginning to repent of their decision. According to the chief's statement, they professed themselves unable to leave off what had been such a strong and universal custom among them for ages. I was told. . .that the head chief of the Indians is going to ask me to give up my school for about a month, his complaint being that the children running past his house and from school tended to unsettle him and his party from working their mysteries. . . . I see now that, although I have been as careful as possible not to give unnecessary offence, yet a storm is on the horizon.

As I went through part of the camp on my way to the school this morning, I met a strong medicine party full in the face. . . . Their naked prodigy was carrying a dead dog, which he occasionally laid down and feasted upon. While a little boy was striking the steel for me at school, some of the party made their appearance near the school, I imagine, for all at once the boy begun to be irregular and feeble in his stroke, and when I looked up at him, I saw he was looking very much afraid. On enquiring the cause, he told me the medicine folks were near; I told him to strike away and I stood at the door of the school. Some few stragglers of the medicine party were hovering about but they did not dare to interfere with us. When all were assembled and the striking ceased, my adult pupils commenced a great talk. . . . After a little time the chief came and told me the Indians were talking bad outside, by which I understood that the medicine folks had been using more threats to stop us. . . .

The leading topics of the chief's clamour I may class as follows: He requested four days' suspension of the school. He promised that if I complied, he and his people would then come to school; but threatened, if my pupils continued to come on the following days, he would shoot at them. Lastly, he pleaded that if the school went on during the time he specified then some medicine men, whom he expected on a visit shortly from a distant tribe, would shame and perhaps kill him. Some of his sayings during his fits of rage were that he understood how to kill people, occasionally drawing his hand across his throat to show me what he meant; that when he died, he should go down; he could not change; he could not be good; or if I made him good, why then he supposed he should go to a different place from his forefathers; this he did not desire to do.

On one occasion, while he was talking, he looked at two men — one of them a regular pupil of mine, and the other a medicine man — and said, "I am a murderer, and so are you, and you (pointing to each of these men); and what good is it for us to come to school?"

R.C. Mayne

Schoolchildren, Metlakatla, North-west Coast, B.C., 1881. Photo by: Edward Dossetter

Kwah Kwelth girls, Knight Inlet, North-west Coast, B.C., 1881. Photo by: Edward Dossetter

These Indian women had been most serviceable to us in dressing skins and heads, drying meat, and mending or making clothes; so, when adding a small present to the mere payment for their work, I was glad to find among my stores a parcel of beads exactly to their taste. It amused me to see that fashion reigned here as imperiously as in more civilized lands; some fine, richly-coloured, oval beads the size of pigeon's eggs, which I considered my best, and which a year or two before would have been generally admired, were despised and out of date, while the little trashy white ones, no bigger than a pin's head, were highly appreciated. Perhaps the small beads were valued as useful for embroidery, in which the Indian and halfbreed women excel; while the larger ones, only serving for necklaces and ornaments, had come to be thought too barbaric by those who lived at the forts.

James Carnegie, Earl of Southesk

160

Ornament

Some also wear a piece of bone inside the lower lip.... Preparation for this, of course, has to be commenced while the "patient" is young: they first bore a hole in the hollow of the under lip, in which is put a piece of silver the shape of a pen. After some time this is taken out and an oval-shaped piece of wood inserted horizontally; after a time this becomes too small, and a larger piece is inserted till, as a woman gets towards old age, she will have a piece of wood three inches long and two inches wide in the lip.... The lip-piece is concave on both sides, while the edge is grooved so as to keep it in its place; this sometimes answers the purpose of a spoon, and Mr. Duncan says he has seen an old woman put her food on it for a few seconds while it cooled and then, raising her lip, empty this semi-natural platter into her mouth. This lip, he says, is considered a mark of honour among these poor creatures: a woman's rank among women — that is, as far as her word, opinion, or advice is concerned — is settled according to the size of her wooden lip; so that if a young woman dares to quarrel with an old one, the latter will not remind her of her youth, inexperience, and consequent unfitness to dictage to age, but will reproach her with the inferior size of her lip.

R.C. Mayne

Haida woman, Yan, Queen Charlotte Islands, B.C., 1881.
Photo by: Edward Dossetter

161

Potlatch

October 23rd — We had a grand festival amongst the Indians, several tribes coming to a feast here. These festivals are annual, held at different places and the chiefs give away presents; he who can give the most being considered the greatest. Some gave away between three and 400 blankets besides guns and other things, absolutely reducing themselves to poverty; the chiefs were seated on high scaffolds and threw blankets to the crowd beneath who were armed with long poles on which they tried to catch the blankets and then a regular scramble ensued, some of the blankets were quite torn to pieces by the scramblers. It was a very exciting scene and recalled the old football rushes at school and I felt a strong inclination to join in and try my chance.

Charles Wilson

Conjuror

There are Indian conjurors who will allow themselves to be bound from head to foot with nets, cords, straps, or anything; then, entering their small "medicine tent," it is seen to heave violently for about five minutes, after which all the fastenings are thrown out at the top of the tent, not one knot being disturbed, and the wizard steps forth perfectly free.... Angus McKay once tied a leaf of a Bible in the net, and the conjuror presently declared he could do nothing till it was taken away.

James Carnegie, Earl of Southesk

Masks

During the course of the evening, and after supper, we were entertained by the exhibition of a native dance, in which some fifty men and women participated. They came trooping in, nearly all masked and dressed in the most curious attire; the men divested of their nether garments, and the women rather scantily arrayed considering the time of the year. To describe the dance would be impossible. The motions were vigorous and, if not graceful, were at any rate whimsical and rather free; the men and women dancing alternately. During the intervals of the dance I examined some of the masks, which were beautifully made. They were of all styles and represented the faces of different animals. I was much struck with one, a delicately carved wooden imitation of an eagle's head, with a rather exaggerated beak and movable eyes, which, during the most vigorous part of the dance, rolled about in a manner fearful to contemplate.

Charles Horetzky

Death

When the fish was eaten, the strangers put a kettle of rice on the fire; the Indians looked at each other, and whispered "Akshahn, akshahn!" or, "Maggots, maggots!" The rice being cooked, some molasses was produced and mixed with it. The Indians stared and said, "Coutree um tsakah ahket," or "The grease of dead people." The whites then tendered the rice and molasses to the Indians, but they only shrank away in disgust. Seeing this, to prove their integrity, they sat down and enjoyed it themselves. The sight stunned the Indians, and again they all "died". Some other similar wonders were worked, and the profound stupor which the Indians felt each time to come over them they termed death.

The Indians' turn had now come to make the white strangers die; they dressed their heads and painted their faces. A "nok-nok" or "wonder-working spirit" possessed them: they came slowly and solemnly, seated themselves before the whites, then suddenly lifted up their heads and stared; their reddened eyes had the desired effect — the whites died.

R.C. Mayne

Greatness

A nation to be great must have great thoughts; must be inspired with lofty ideals; must have men and women willing to work and wait and war "for an idea." To be a light to the dark places of the earth; to rule inferior races mercifully and justly; to infuse into them a higher life; to give them "the good news" that makes men blessed and free, believing that as the race is one, reason one, and conscience one, there is one Gospel for and unto all; nothing less than this was the thought — deeply felt if sometimes inarticulately expressed — of our great ancestors in the brave days of Old. And it is ours also.

George Grant

Haida Indians, Masset, Queen Charlotte Islands, B.C., 1881. Photo by: Edward Dossetter

Indian graves at Salmon River, North-west Coast, B.C., 1881. Photo by: Edward Dossetter

164